The Road of Hope

THE ROAD
of HOPE

a gospel from prison

By
Francis Xavier Nguyễn Văn Thuận

Official English Edition

Pauline
BOOKS & MEDIA
Boston

Library of Congress Cataloging-in-Publication Data

Francis Xavier Nguyễn Văn Thuận, 1928–
  [Duong hy vong. English]
  The road of hope: a gospel from prison / by F.X. Nguyễn Văn Thuận.
    p. cm.
  ISBN 0-8198-6473-0 (pbk.)
    1. Meditations. 2. Christian life—Catholic authors. I. Title.
  BX2187.V54 N4913 2001
  248.4'82—dc21
                                                        2001004543

Texts of the New Testament used in this work are taken from *The New Testament: St. Paul Catholic Edition* translated by Mark A. Wauck, copyright © 2000, by the Society of St. Paul, Staten Island, New York, and are used by permission. All rights reserved.

Texts of the Old Testament are from *The New Revised Standard Version Bible: Catholic Edition,* copyright © 1993 and 1989 by the Division of Christian Education of the National Council of the Churches of Christ in the U.S.A. Used by permission. All rights reserved.

ISBN 0-8198-6473-0

Originally published in Vietnamese under the title *Duong Hy Vong* by the Federation of Vietnamese Catholics, Chicago, IL.

Translated by Peter Bookallil

Adapted with author's permission by Linda Salvatore Boccia, FSP and Madonna Therese Ratliff, FSP

Cover art and design by Helen Rita Lane, FSP

Printed and published in the U.S.A. by Pauline Books & Media, 50 Saint Pauls Avenue, Boston, MA 02130-3491.

www.pauline.org

Pauline Books & Media is the publishing house of the Daughters of St. Paul, an international congregation of women religious serving the Church with the communications media.

2 3 4 5 6 7 8 9   07 06 05 04 03

Contents

Biographical Sketch of
Francis Xavier Nguyễn Văn Thuận

- Francis Xavier Nguyễn Văn Thuận was born on April 17, 1928, in Huề, Vietnam. As a boy, Văn Thuận participated in the various activities of the Catholic movement, *Eucharistic Crusade,* and discovered a priestly vocation. He entered the seminary in Huề and was ordained a priest in June 1953.

- From 1956 to 1959, Văn Thuận studied in Rome, receiving his doctorate in canon law from what is now the Pontifical University Urbaniana. Upon returning to Vietnam, he was asked to teach at the seminary and later became its Rector and Vicar General.

- In 1967, Pope Paul VI named Văn Thuận bishop of Nha Trang, a position he held for eight years. During this time, Văn Thuận focused his attention on priestly vocations and the theological formation of both clergy and laity. He served as chairman to the Vietnamese Episcopal Conference for social communications and development, and collaborated in founding Radio Veritas, Asia's Catholic broadcast network. In 1971, he joined the Pontifical Council of the Laity, and at the request of Paul VI, traveled widely to solicit aid for the reconstruction of Vietnam.

• On April 23, 1975, Văn Thuận was named Titular Archbishop of Vadesi and Coadjutor Archbishop of Saigon in South Vietnam. But only three months later Bishop Văn Thuận was taken into custody and held in the parish church of a small village where he was placed in solitary confinement on March 18, 1976.

• On December 1, 1976, the Archbishop and 1,500 other prisoners were sent to North Vietnam where Văn Thuận was held in a number of "re-education camps." Nine years of his imprisonment were spent in various isolation cells.

• On November 21, 1988, the Archbishop was formally released from prison, but kept under house arrest in Hanoi for three years, thus preventing him from any pastoral activity.

• In December 1991, Văn Thuận was expelled from Vietnam and went to Rome.

• On November 24, 1994, Archbishop Văn Thuận was made Vice President of the Pontifical Council for Justice and Peace. On June 24, 1998, he became its President.

• In 2001, Francis Xavier Nguyễn Văn Thuận was named a Cardinal by Pope John Paul II.

While incarcerated in Vietnam, Bishop Văn Thuận was prevented from ministering to his people. However, despite his confinement, he refused to remain passive. During his nights in prison, before being placed in solitary confinement, Văn Thuận recorded his thoughts as encouraging messages to his people. These brief reflections, scribbled on scraps of paper torn from old calendars, were smuggled out of prison by a young boy who visited Văn Thuận every day. The boy took these messages home to his brothers and sisters who copied them by hand and then circulated them among the faithful. Bishop Văn Thuận was thus able to remain with his people in a hidden yet powerful way during their time of need.

The Road of Hope is the collection of these 1,001 thoughts, a true "gospel from prison," written to console and strengthen a weary people in their faith. The messages remain the heartfelt, personal words of a father who sustained and nourished his children in their desire for freedom. Today they speak to us—an invitation to begin our own journey on the Road of Hope that leads us to our future.

The Road of Hope

"In this piece of art, think of the bamboos as our lives. The bent bamboos look like they are suffering under a strong wind. They represent difficult times. The mountains loom on the horizon. They represent God in the three Divine Persons. The road that is formed by the strong, enduring, yet flexible bamboos leads to God, our Savior, our hope." — Hai Nam Nguyen, artist

CHAPTER 1

Departure

*If you are still bound with a gold chain,
you are not ready for this road.*

1   Our Lord is guiding you on a road so that you will "go out and bear fruit, and that your fruit should abide " (Jn 15:16). This road is called the Road of Hope because it overflows with hope and is as beautiful as hope itself. Why shouldn't you have hope as you begin to take this road on the way to the Father with our Lord Jesus Christ himself?

2   The journey along this Road of Hope has three stages:

1) Departure: "Renounce yourself";
2) God's Will: "Take up your cross daily";
3) Perseverance: "Follow me" (cf. Lk 9:23).

3   If you give up everything, but still do not deny yourself, you actually have not given up anything at all.

You will gradually gather again to yourself all those things you gave up in the first place.

4   Abraham set out on his journey because he hoped to reach the Promised Land. Moses likewise set out because he hoped to rescue God's people from slavery. Our Lord Jesus Christ came down from heaven with the hope of saving all humanity.

5   If you leave your home and go to a distant place, perhaps even thousands of miles away, but continue to bring along all your bad habits and the "old self" of sin, what difference does it make?

6   The saints are fools for Christ (cf. 1 Cor 4:10). The making of saints is far beyond the scope of this world's wisdom.

7   If you wish to set off on this road, you must go regardless of what other people say to ridicule you. The three Magi set out with the hope of meeting the Savior, and they met him. Francis Xavier set out with the hope of bringing the Gospel to people, and he met them. Maria Goretti set out to resist temptation with the hope of meeting our Lord, and she met him.

8   You must lose in order to gain, die in order to live, abandon everything in order to meet the Lord. The Magi risked both dangers and ridicule; Francis Xavier left his parents and gave up all his possessions; Maria Goretti gave up her life.

9   Keep advancing along the Road of Hope regardless of the heartrending pleas of those you love. Paul knew that "bondage and affliction" awaited him (cf. Acts 20:23), and Jesus said, "Now I must go up to Jerusalem to suffer" (cf. Mt 16:21), yet they continued along the road marked out for them.

10   It doesn't matter at all whether you are rich or poor, whether people praise you or ridicule you, whether you are of noble or humble status, so long as you are determined to advance along this road and wait in joyful hope for the coming of our Savior Jesus Christ.

11   The Lord says, "I am the way and the truth" (Jn 14:6). He doesn't say that everything in the newspapers is the truth, that all radio or television shows are the truth. What kind of truth will you follow?

12   Keep moving forward relentlessly; do not give up. No one follows the person who turns back.

13   Do not yield to lustfulness, to laziness, to selfishness. You cannot call black white, bad good, or dishonesty honesty.

14   Are you a person who says "yes" to everything? Do you say "yes" to many gods and a variety of moral standards? Do you have a permissive conscience that adjusts to any situation and says "yes" to passing values? What road will you take?

15   To refuse to give in to false values is not pride, egoism, or stubbornness; rather, it is proof of your whole-hearted adherence to true standards and values.

16   Be prepared to reject wealth and position — even to give up your own life — in order to preserve your ideals, your integrity, and your faith. You must never behave otherwise, for to do so means to lose everything.

CHAPTER 2
God's Will

God's will is the passport to heaven.

17   Your responsibilities indicate the will of God for you at the present moment.

18   There are some people who will not carry their own cross or anyone else's, yet they still imagine that their cross is too heavy. Some are eager to take everyone else's cross upon their shoulders, but they refuse to carry their own.

19   Make your responsibilities holy and help others to holiness through them. Grow in holiness by the way you carry out your mission in life.

20   If everyone were faithful to their responsibilities in life, their growth in personal holiness would renew their own hearts and would bring about a like renewal in families and in the whole world.

21　　Despite superficial appearances, a person who neglects his or her responsibilities in life is a false saint. Even if he or she worked "miracles," these would be out of place and become a cause of confusion. Moreover, such a person would be a burden to live with.

22　　Some people mistakenly believe that holiness consists simply in methods of prayer, preaching, or in withdrawal from "the world" taken from the examples of priests and religious of former times. On the other hand, there are those who conceive holiness only in terms of social and political activity; what is needed is both prayer and action.

23　　Because people often conceive of holiness as something outside their ordinary responsibilities, the world is not renewed.

24　　The worker will become a saint in the workplace, the soldier will become a saint in the army, the patient will become a saint in the hospital, the student will become a saint through studies, the farmer will become a saint on the farm, the priest will become a saint through his ministry as a priest, and the public servant will become a saint in the government office. Every step on the road to holiness is a step of sacrifice in the performance of one's mission in life.

25　　It is not for acts of prophecy or the performance of miracles that saints become saints. They do not do anything extraordinary, they simply carry out their ordinary activities.

26   However, the mission of the present moment is not a passive thing. It is an unceasing renewal of yourself, it is a decision to choose the Lord, it is a search for the kingdom of God, and a belief in the infinite love of God. It is acting with all the ardor of your heart and of reflecting that love of God by means of your love for others right at this present moment.

27   God's will is your passport to heaven: "The one who does the will of my Father in heaven will enter the kingdom of heaven" (cf. Mt 7:21).

28   Accept the will of God, obey the will of God, love the will of God...which way will you choose?

29   If you happen to endure some disgrace because of your mission in life, at that moment you share the burden of the Lord's cross.

30   Let your response be, "O Lord, my mission has brought me to Calvary; I am a holocaust."

31   To become a saint, it is only necessary for you to fulfill your present responsibility. The discovery and revelation of this fact will bring peace and encouragement to your soul.

32   In fact, your death will be your last "obligation," and you must accept it willingly and in a manner filled with love.

33   As you advance in carrying out your everyday responsibilities, you will come to appreciate that "our

Lord's yoke is easy, and his burden light" (cf. Mt 11:30).

34   Your soul is worried and discontented because you set conditions on the performance of your mission or because you place limitations on following the will of God.

35   If you are not attached to the will of God moment by moment, you may begin to think of your daily activities as too uneventful, unnoticed, and monotonous. Then you will fall by the wayside on the Road of Hope.

36   The solution to this problem is very simple. Before doing anything, ask: "What should I do, Lord?" (Acts 22:10). Then carry out the will of God.

37   When God desires it to rain, do you desire the same? When God desires it to be sunny, do you desire the same? When God desires things to be pleasant, do you desire the same? When God allows things to be difficult, do you accept the same? When God allows that you endure some suffering, do you accept the same? This is the secret of happiness: to have but one will with God.

38   In our daily life the Lord gives us the happiness of participating in the mystery of redemption. For each person, the road of the cross lies along the road of their mission in life.

CHAPTER 3

Perseverance

Anyone can begin, but only
the saints continue to the end.

39   If you desire to reach the end of this Road of Hope, you must be fearless, and to be fearless means not wandering about aimlessly. How many people stood beside our Lord at the foot of the cross?

40   Don't be afraid to tell the Lord about everything you desire. Remember his words: "Up till now you have asked for nothing in my name; ask and you will receive" (Jn 16:24). To be fearless means loving just as a child loves his or her father.

41   Don't be discouraged by your failures. When you seek to do the will of God and meet with failure, that failure may be a success in God's eyes because the outcome is as God desired. Look at the example of Jesus on the cross.

42   Results and success are very different things. Perhaps there are no outward results but instead there is an increase in experience, in humility, in your faith in God. That is your success from a spiritual point of view.

43   There is only one failure: not to hope in God. "Hope in God and you will not be disappointed" (cf. Ps 22:5).

44   Don't be an erratic saint: a sudden storm could wipe away appearances to reveal an inner reality of sinfulness.

45   The virtuous person exudes a sweet perfume quietly and unobtrusively.

46   Exercise loyalty along the road you are traveling. Peter did not betray the Lord or accuse him. But neither did Peter support the Lord by so much as a single word. He said, "I do not know the man" (Mt 26:72), seeking to remain safe and to avoid being implicated. Peter lost hope in the Lord as the Way, and he fled from him.

47   You may tremble with fear, you may stumble and fall, you might meet with difficulties, misunderstandings, criticism, disgrace, perhaps even a death sentence. But why forget the Gospel? Our Lord Jesus Christ suffered everything. If you continue to follow him, you will also have your Easter.

48   Each morning when you get up, you begin life anew — fresh, energetic, and full of optimism. If the road runs badly at times, continue to walk along with

the Lord just as the disciples did on the road to Emmaus, and you will reach the goal.

49   Perseverance is a characteristic of the saints, because "whoever holds out till the end, they will be saved" (Mt 10:22).

50   Even if everyone else falls by the wayside on the journey, you must press forward. A leader who guides wisely is rare indeed and large numbers of people are easily seduced by someone who leads unwisely. You must have the strength of character not to follow the crowd blindly.

51   Though you might feel worn-out or less enthusiastic, keep your spirits up. Dark clouds pass and won't continue to block out the sunlight. Just wait for the clouds to pass.

52   Don't say, "I lack inspiration." Is your work the result of personal inspiration alone? The work of God is not comparable to writing poetry. Work because of love and with the knowledge of the fact that you will never lose God's love.

53   The good thief achieved happiness because of his hope in God's love (cf. Mt 27:5).

54   In his darkest hour of desolation, Jesus cried out: "My God, my God, why have You forsaken me?" (Mt 27:46); at that moment his mother Mary stood by the cross. She was silent, but her steadfast love was great

enough to support her son until he said, "All has been fulfilled" (Jn 19:30).

55   Though the body of the widow of Naim's son was being carried out for burial (cf. Lk 7:12), and the body of the dead Lazarus was already decaying in the grave (cf. Jn 11:39), our Lord still called them both to rise from the dead. Have hope and humbly repent of your sins; the Lord will also raise you up.

56   Each day you must decrease in self-centeredness and increase in love of neighbor. Each day, decrease in self-reliance and instead increase your trust in God.

57   If you lack determination to persevere, you cannot say, "I am meek"; say rather, "I am a coward."

58   You keep complaining: "If only I were in that particular place, working with that particular person, or holding that particular office I would certainly be successful." No! Do the work the Lord has entrusted to you. You are exactly where he has placed you; go straight ahead. If you rush about in all directions you will not reach the goal.

59   When you strive to persevere, you are imitating the loyal, faithful John. When you cowardly abandon the struggle, you choose the way of the traitor, Judas.

60   But, you say, "It's too difficult!" This is true. Still, only what is acquired through effort is really worthwhile.

CHAPTER 4

Religious Vocation

*Mobilize all your strength
to follow God's call.*

61 "Follow me, and I will make you fish for people!"
(Mt 4:19). The apostles gave up everything to follow
the Lord. Like them, are you going to decide immediately to follow him when he calls? If not, then how
many times will he have to call you?

62 Making decisions always involves some uncer-
tainty. Hesitate and ponder as you will; in the end you
will still have to make a decision.

63 Jesus clearly states the drastic measures he requires:
"If any want to be my disciple, let them deny themselves, take up their cross daily and follow me" (Lk
9:23); and "Whoever comes to me and does not hate
father and mother and wife and children, brothers and
sisters, even life itself, cannot be my disciple" (Lk

14:26). The road to follow has been clearly defined and the call is unambiguous.

64   "Go into the whole world and proclaim the good news to all creation" (Mk 16:15). Of those who dare to accept this lofty mission our Lord requires a readiness to die, that is, a fearlessness in the face of death. If we look over the Church's two-thousand-year history, we see that in every age, and from every class of people, there has never been a lack of those willing to die for the Gospel.

65   There are some people who rely on everyone else to make their decisions. Are you one of those people?

66   Perhaps you wish to retreat because of setbacks or because you met people who could not endure the various difficulties and trials they encountered. But will you follow our Lord or those others?

67   Why are you so surprised that there are many who follow the call of the Lord and are even willing to die? Remember the Lord's words, "and, behold, I will be with you all the days until the end of the age" (Mt 28:20).

68   Some people will never understand why we follow the Lord's call. They think we are crazy, but people also thought that Jesus was crazy; we should be proud to share in such divine insanity.

69   Your decision to follow the Lord is not just a matter of signing your name on a document or of pronouncing vows. There is the continuous day-by-day sacrifice involved in living such a decision throughout your whole life.

70   "You see we have left everything and followed you; what will there be for us, then?" (Mt 19:27). You have given up everything to follow the Lord who is your protector. Why are you still worrying?

71   While you are following the Lord, do not be surprised if you should hear the call of pleasure, of esteem, of your body, of family, or of the temptation to abandon this road. Continue onward, remembering the Lord's warning, "No one who puts his hand to the plow and looks behind is fit for the kingdom of God" (Lk 9:62).

72   "Follow me!" (Mt 9:9). This call continues to remind you of your commitment through all the little tasks that you perform, and your "yes" must continue until your last breath.

73   To respond "yes" is easy, but see how the Lord followed his call up to his death on the cross. You must deny yourself, carry your cross every day, and nail yourself to that cross.

74   The Lord commands you, "Go into the whole world and proclaim the good news to all creation" (Mk 16:15), but he doesn't issue a timetable or draw up a plan. He

leaves the initiative — and the difficulties to be overcome — to you, and asks only that you carry the Gospel
wherever you go.

75   The Second Vatican Council teaches us to return to
the sources, rediscovering the lives of the apostles, the
people who lived with Jesus, those who listened to him,
who had personal contact with him, and who witnessed
to him.

76   A program that is going ahead well often has to be
left unfinished; some zealous efforts are restrained,
some intense activities are scaled down, and you may
become upset and discouraged. But has the Lord called
you to follow him, or this work or that person? Leave
everything to the Lord and he will work things out for
the best.

77   You don't trust anyone, you don't delegate work to
anyone, you don't give up your position to anyone…are
you more powerful than God himself, who has allowed
us to share in his work?

78   Why do you keep such a hold over this or that work
and refuse to let it go when you are asked to move on to
other duties? The work belongs to the Lord more than
to you; it is his concern.

79   The moment you experience self-satisfaction in
your ministry is the most dangerous moment. This is
when the devil will concentrate all his forces to take
you by surprise.

CHAPTER 5

The Interior Life

*The contemplative life
is realized in your actions.*

80   Peace depends on victory, and victory depends on struggle. If you desire peace, you will have to fight continuously.

81   Your "weapons" in this struggle are meditation, self-denial, the sacraments, the rosary, and recollection. Your allies are Mary, Joseph, the angels, your patron saints, and your spiritual director. Unless you gradually drop your weapons or betray your allies, your victory is assured.

82   If you stand on the top of a tall building and look down onto the street below, you will see streams of people running in all directions — fighting and quarrelling with each other, frantically rushing around in circles, all for the sake of love or money, ambition or

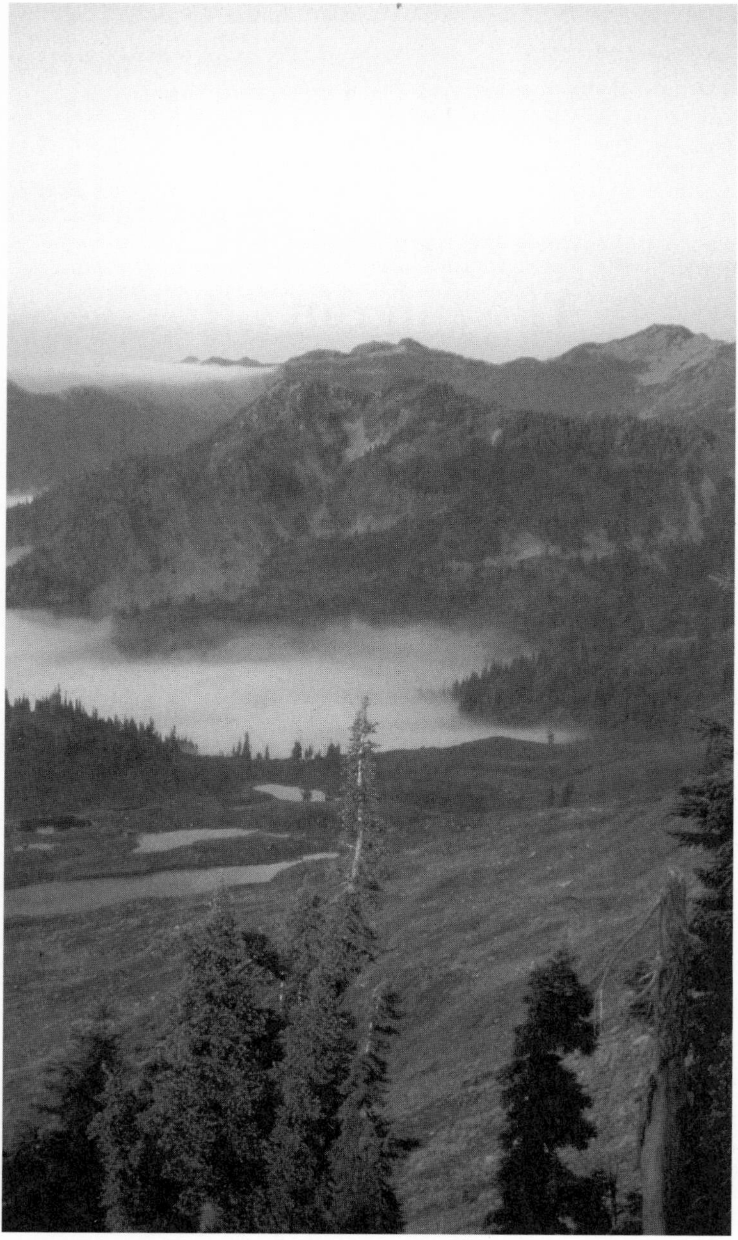

competition. Only when we throw as much of ourselves into the work of God without any fear will we have a faith that is alive and a passionate apostolic spirit.

83   If you were determined to practice one virtue every year, and you practiced it every day, very soon you would make quite an improvement.

84   As a diver or astronaut launches out adventurously for the cause of science, so you can do no less. When you give up everything for the Lord, even risking your life for him, then the authenticity of your interior life will be evident to others.

85   You wish to set fire to the whole world with the love the Gospel preaches; you wish to conquer the five continents. Then your every moment should be a flash of fire — the fire of your mission, your obedience, and your patience. Such a flame will burn brightly to illuminate the whole world.

86   External and, even more, inner silence is the atmosphere most helpful to the interior life.

87   You do not have to be educated or extraordinarily talented to become holy. All you require is the grace of God and your own determination. Few people become saints, because it is easier to become educated than it is to make the necessary changes in one's life to become holy.

88   Although you are eager to serve God well, if such enthusiasm is not accompanied by a deep personal renewal, this will not be pleasing to God.

89   Some people are afraid of silence because they feel empty. People who consciously live an interior life, instead, value silence because they discover a new and beautiful world in a life of intimacy with the Blessed Trinity, a life which this world cannot give.

90   If you had done your utmost in the past to eliminate one bad habit each year, correcting yourself a little every day, by now you would have fewer faults and imperfections.

91   You ask when you must begin to live a more intense interior life. Begin at this very moment, and begin again each and every day.

92   Who must become holy? Everyone without exception must become holy, because God calls everyone. But begin with yourself.

93   There is nothing as precious as divine grace. With it heaven reigns in your heart even here in this life.

94   A precious, sparkling diamond is formed in a mass of rock, hidden in the depths of the earth, over millions of years. Do you emerge from your time of prayer in the same way?

95   Spread throughout the world and proclaim in a loud voice, "There is one man who has laid down his life for his friends" (cf. Jn 15:13; 1 Cor 15:3; 2 Cor 5:14–15; 1 Thes 5:9–10).

96   A raging fire pictured in a film can frighten the audience, but it's a fire that doesn't burn hot. Neither can it cook, because it is only an image; it does not come forth from a red hot furnace.

97   Our love of God has to be absolute. The Lord teaches us that "no one can serve two masters" (Mt 6:24). How many masters do you serve?

98   Set aside a few quiet moments every day to help you to advance in your interior life. How many minutes have you set aside lately?

99   Some people say there is a crisis of faith or of authority, but I think there is actually a crisis of holiness. Any trials you encounter can refine you and separate the good from the bad in you.

100   Augustine says in his prayer, "Lord, let me know you, let me know myself." His words are better understood alongside the Lord's question, "Have I been with you so long, and yet you do not recognize me, Philip?" (Jn 14:9). If you *know* truly, your life will change completely.

101   There are people whose religious practice consists of reciting many prayers and participating in many Eucharistic Celebrations, but they do not put their faith into practice. It is the same as someone asking a friend, "Are you well?" and the friend replying, "I eat six meals a day." Eating many meals is not necessarily the same thing as being healthy.

CHAPTER 6

The
Supernatural Life

*The supernatural life consists in a
wholehearted commitment to the will of God.*

102   If everyone but God approves of you, how terrible!
If everyone insults you, falsely accuses you, or perse-
cutes you, but God praises you, how happy are you, for
the kingdom of heaven is yours (cf. Lk 6:22).

103   Of what use is it if everyone should affirm you, but
God disapproves? If everyone mocks you, but God affirms you, happy are you! When the crowd cried out,
"Release Barabbas to us!" (Lk 23:18), Barabbas remained a robber just the same. When the crowd cried
out, "Crucify him!" (Lk 23:21), Jesus was still the
sinless Son of God.

104   When you are faced with the ingratitude of people
who have betrayed and falsely accused you, what hurts

most is the irrational malice that pours out of those from whom you least expect it. In such circumstances this should be your reaction: to forgive from the heart, to beg for God's forgiveness for your enemies, and to pray with love for their conversion. In this way you will not need to rely on the consolation of the world.

105   Rejoice at your success, but thank God when someone else is more successful than you.

106   What is foolishness in the eyes of others is wisdom in the eyes of God (cf. 1 Cor 1:22–24; Gal 6:14).

107   The cross of Christ was foolishness to the Jews and a stumbling block to the Greeks, but we glory in it (cf. 1 Cor 1:22–24; Gal 6:14).

108   To spend the whole day in church does not necessarily make you holy if at the same time you continue to criticize others, to react according to the wisdom of "the world," or to be self-centered. The apostles John and James were with Jesus often, yet he had to rebuke them (cf. Lk 9:55).

109   Do not easily say, "I follow my conscience." Are you sure of the conscience you follow?

110   Poverty, obedience, mortification, meekness, charity, forgiveness, and humility are all foolishness in the eyes of "the world," but supremely important in the eyes of God. What "the world" regards as misfortune, God considers true happiness.

111   Look at everything from God's point of view and you will see things differently.

112   In all your activities and struggles, try to discern how to act by asking yourself: how much desire do I have to do God's will? And how much desire to fulfill your own will, to seek personal advantage, or to satisfy self-love? Perhaps you will discover very little of God in your endeavors.

113   "I planted, Apollos watered, but it was God who caused the growth" (1 Cor 3:6).

114   If there is no resurrection, Christians are the most unfortunate people in the world (cf. 1 Cor 15:14, 17, 19).

115   When you proclaim that you work "for God and for the Church," stand silently in God's presence and ask honestly, "Lord, do you see that I am working completely for you? You are the essential object of all that I do and I would be ashamed to admit any other motive."

116   Since you have dedicated yourself to the service of God, why do you still compare your life to that of others and complain about your inferior circumstances? Do you regret serving God because of the losses that you suffer?

117   The seventy-two disciples rejoiced that even the demons were subject to them in the Lord's name. But Jesus reminded them not to rejoice so much over the performance of a miracle as in the fact that their names were written in heaven. You should also rejoice more over the Lord's promise of heaven than over any "miracles" you may perform (cf. Lk 10:17–20).

CHAPTER 7
Prayer

My vocation is to pray.

118   Action without prayer is useless in the sight of God — otherwise, a robot could do more than you.

119   Prayer is of prime importance in our lives; second is sacrifice; and only in third place is activity.

120   Prayer is the very foundation of the spiritual life. When you pray you are in communication with God, just as a lightbulb glows when connected to electricity.

121   You believe that prayer is all-powerful, don't you? Consider the Lord's words, "Ask! and it shall be given to you; seek! and you shall find; knock! and it shall be opened to you" (Lk 11:9). Can any insurance company give a more certain guarantee?

122   Prayer is the secret of nurturing the Christian life. Do not believe in someone who performs a miracle, but does not pray.

123   Pray always and everywhere. Jesus tells us that we ought "to pray always" (Lk 18:1) and "pray that you will not come to the test" (Mt 26:41).

124   "For where two or three are gathered in my name, I am there among them" (Mt 18:20). These words of the Lord are fulfilled especially in those many communities that have no priest, yet continue to organize themselves to pray together and hold firmly to this practice despite their difficulties and isolation.

125   Are you surprised that there are many people who have lost the grace of God, lost their faith, or have turned against the Church? There are many reasons for this, but there will always be one main reason: lack of prayer.

126   Do not neglect vocal prayer. When the apostles asked Jesus to teach them how to pray, he replied, "Pray like this: Our Father Who art in heaven" (Mt 6:9); Jesus taught them vocal prayer.

127   You are taught to recite prayers in order to help you to pray, but prayer itself is the encounter and conversation between Father and child. "When you pray, go into your room and shut the door; pray to your Father Who is hidden, and your Father Who sees what's hidden will reward you" (Mt 6:6). There is no need to be formal; simply pray from the heart as a child speaks to his or her father.

128   The prayers of the liturgy are very pleasing to God because they come from the words of Scripture and the prayers of the Church, which is the Body of Christ. Use a missal, a book of the psalms, or a prayer book to help you to pray.

129   It is not without foundation that I say, "Prayer is of prime importance." Jesus told us, "Mary has chosen the better part, which will not be taken from her" (Lk 10:42). As she sat at the Lord's feet, listening to his words lovingly, Mary had in Jesus all that we now have in the Eucharist, Sacred Scripture, and the whole of liturgical prayer.

130   You seek a friend to comfort you and ease your loneliness. Why not look for a friend who will never let you down, one who will stay with you always, no matter where you may be?

131   A seemingly holy person who does not pray is not a saint. Wait and see, the mask will crumble before long.

132   You can judge the effectiveness of a person's ministry by looking at his or her prayer life.

133   If you are not a person of prayer, no one will believe that you work for God alone.

134   Why are there crises in the Church? It is because people do not take prayer seriously.

135   Our prayer should be as fervent as the prayer of Mary and the apostles in the upper room before Pentecost, as trusting as that of Jesus in the Garden of Olives, as resolute as that of Moses when he stretched out his arms on the mountain as the battle raged, and as confident of forgiveness as that of the good thief.

136   "Not by bread alone shall you live, but by every utterance proceeding from the mouth of God" (Mt 4:4), that is: the Eucharist, Scripture, and liturgical prayer. Without these, there is no spiritual life.

137   Prayer on the lips of an unbeliever is a genuine sign of the beginnings of faith.

138   The spirit of prayer is similar to a furnace burning in your apostolic soul. If you wish to feed that fire, you must stir up the larger logs of sacrifice and recollection as well as the kindling of frequent brief prayers and secret acts of self-denial.

139   Even if you do not utter a word, God understands your heart completely. Look at the example in the Gospel of the woman who had suffered from a "chronic bleeding for twelve years." As soon as she touched the hem of the Lord's garment, she was immediately cured without so much as a word (cf. Mt 9:21; Mk 5:28; Lk 8:44).

140   As a sinner, you might not dare to stand in the presence of God. Yet, the words of the Church's prayer: "Through Christ our Lord" should reassure you. Do you think that all the sufferings of Jesus and all the good works of his Mother and the saints are not sufficient to encompass your little prayers?

141   Do you think that children are not yet able to do anything for the Church, or that the sick can no longer do anything for the Church? This is not at all the case. After the official prayer of the Church, it is the prayers of children and the sick which are most pleasing to God. Remind them often of this.

142   Your times of prayer are moments of intimacy with God, who is your Father. Prayer is not like writing an essay; it is a time for the heart, not the head. Do not rack your brains or scratch your head over how you should address God.

143   There are many places in the world without priests, yet the people have maintained the faith by means of family prayer.

144   Your prayer should encompass everyone; your heart should include the entire world. But do not forget your personal realities and those around you.

145   Spiritual books have helped many people to become saints. They are the oil that fuels the furnace of prayer.

146   In a particular way, cloistered religious should declare on their identification cards: "Occupation: Prayer." The world needs the prayers of these men and women religious.

147   It was not laziness that made Mary sit quietly at the Lord's feet. Mary chose the better part: to listen to the Lord and allow his words to permeate her heart and soul and — working in and with her — to effect a change. What could be more active than interior renewal and transformation?

CHAPTER 8

Sacrifice

Sacrifice is the proof of love.

148   Sacrifice and contemplative prayer go hand in hand. If you do not practice sacrifice, do not complain that your prayer has grown cold.

149   You have to make many sacrifices when you live in the midst of people who differ from you politically, socially, and ideologically. But look at the example of Jesus. He who is God chose to live among humanity in thirty-three years of continual sacrifice.

150   If you were being tortured, you could adopt one of two attitudes: "This person is destroying me," or "By this person I am becoming a sacrifice."

151   While everyone else would say, "This person is a cause of misfortune," you could say, "This person is the instrument by which I am being transformed."

152   People venerate those privileged individuals who bear the impression of Christ's five wounds — the stigmata — on their bodies. Yet everyone who reverences God "impresses" these five wounds on their own bodies by means of sacrifice.

153   Perhaps you think you have nothing to sacrifice, but do you reject the opportunities that present themselves? For example, be happy and jovial with someone who ridicules you or tries to make you angry; be silent in the face of false and unjust accusations; show love to a friend who betrays you; do not utter an angry word in retaliation. Every single moment is full of opportunities for sacrifice.

154   Sacrifice in accordance with the spirit of the Gospels (cf. Mt 6:16, 16:6–11; Mk 8:1).

155   A person who truly loves, sacrifices all the time and never speaks about it.

156   If you say that you have no opportunities for sacrifice, this is an indication that you still do not love God.

157   Without sacrifice there will be no holiness. You have to deny yourself and take up your cross before you can follow the Lord. Self-denial is a prerequisite of holiness (cf. Mt 16:27; Mk 8:34, 10:21; Lk 9:23).

158   You must sacrifice yourself, not other people.

159   For the sake of love we are prepared to sacrifice everything: "The world must know that I love the Father, and just as the Father has commanded me, that is what I will do" (Jn 14:31).

160   If you do not practice external sacrifice, no one will believe that you practice interior sacrifice. Mortification of the senses is important.

161   Jesus, "knowing that his hour had come to leave this world for the Father, having loved his own in the world, loved them to the end" (Jn 13:1). That end was the cross. Your own sacrifice must be complete; it must be a complete holocaust if you are to truly love to the end.

162   You must sacrifice whatever separates you from the Lord. Recall his words: "If your eye causes you to sin, pull it out!" (Mk 9:47).

163   Some people are burdened with exceptional crosses, but not many people can willingly accept such sacrifices.

164   If you fail to accept small sacrifices, you will certainly surrender when confronted with great sacrifices.

165   As a strong incentive, offer an intention along with a sacrifice — for example, for a sick person or for areas of the world where the Church is encountering many obstacles and difficulties.

166 The way you begin each day is most important. Rise eagerly each morning and you will carry this enthusiasm throughout the day.

167 Do not be afraid! Reread the Acts of the Apostles; enduring hunger, thirst, poverty, robberies, beatings, shipwreck, false accusations, imprisonment, and even death was the lot of the apostles (cf. 2 Cor 11:25–27). If you are afraid, do not become an apostle!

168 If you practice self-discipline through sacrifice, your soul and body will be like two friends who are united and invincible. But, if you cannot discipline yourself, your soul and body will become two enemies that remain so forever.

169 The person of sacrifice is tolerant with the faults and imperfections of others, but less so with regard to his or her own faults and imperfections.

170 There are some people who make sacrifices, but they want everyone to know about it. There are other people who do not make sacrifices, but they want everyone to believe that they do. There are still others who frequently make sacrifices, but do not want anyone knowing about it.

171 In a solemn pilgrimage with thousands of people, everyone wants to carry the cross at the head of the procession. But in the pilgrimage of our everyday lives, how many people are prepared to carry their own crosses? Indeed, it is difficult to be an unsung hero.

172   The choice is between holiness and sinfulness. Many times, holiness or sinfulness is a moment's choice that requires sacrifice, resulting in victory or defeat.

173   The profession of faith, the Credo, should heighten our appreciation of the Lord's sacrifice: "He was born of the Virgin Mary and became man. For our sake he was crucified under Pontius Pilate; he suffered, died, and was buried." Jesus' sacrifice was his entire life — a sacrifice of oblation.

174   You should be ready to sacrifice your life, to sacrifice your whole existence, because of your overwhelming hope in Jesus Christ. "He rose again in accord with the Scriptures; he ascended into heaven, he will come again in glory...his kingdom will have no end."

175   Do not think that you are the only one who makes sacrifices. Look around — from small children to those elderly women who sacrifice everything to raise their children and grandchildren. You would be amazed to know that there are some poor people who, beneath their tattered clothes, are real heroes.

CHAPTER 9

The Heart

Do not let your heart grow old.

176   Do not offer your heart to God and then look for another's heart to replace it. You are not a surgeon performing heart transplants.

177   The older the saints became, the younger their hearts became.

178   Do not let your heart grow old with the passing of time. Love with a love that grows more intense daily, ever new, ever more pure — that is, with the love that God pours into your heart.

179   Why do you hesitate? If you are bound with even a gold chain, cut yourself loose so that you may make progress along this road. The Lord waits to welcome you at the end of it.

180   Every time you fail, you say, "Oh, if only I had made a strong resolution in the beginning!" I hope you do not keep having these belated regrets.

181   You feel that your heart is wavering. The saints also experienced this feeling, but they used this very feeling to help them, by the grace of God and their own efforts, to become saints.

182   Do you hide from God a heart which all kinds of things struggle to possess, without asking God to accept your heart?

183   Can you hope in the Sacred Heart of Jesus, despite what little you may feel you have to offer?

184   You insist that certain questionable friendships help you, but consider: if you are not progressing on the spiritual journey, such friendships may be burdens that are crushing you.

185   Do you peddle your heart everywhere to all comers, but when you find no buyers, take it to offer it to the Lord?

186   Our Lord wants you to give yourself to him totally, not half-heartedly.

187   Give up everything and you will gain everything, you will save everything. Jesus said, "And when I am lifted up from the earth I will draw all to myself" (Jn 12:32).

188   Do not think that by giving up everything your heart will be cold or your life will be lonely or that you will not be lovable. On the contrary, your heart will glow with the light and warmth of the Sacred Heart of Jesus. Just look at the lives of the saints.

189   The saints gave up everything, but the whole world followed them wherever they went.

190   You are not ready to follow the will of God, yet you allow yourself to be enslaved by many people.

191   Heart or mission: which would you choose? Choose mission and then carry it out with all your heart.

192   To be motivated solely by the emotions in an apostolic work may seem very good, but on closer examination we see that before long, emotions may prevail.

193   Many frivolous attachments chain you and prevent you from rising to better things.

194   What is important is not the number of your activities, but the degree of love which transforms them.

CHAPTER 10
Fortitude

*Resolve to immerse yourself
in one book: the Gospel.
Resolve to follow one ideal:
the life of our Lord Jesus Christ.*

195   God has given you the gift of life. He has also given you the freedom to make your life holy and wonderfully useful. Do not misuse it so that it becomes stunted and a betrayal of God's gift.

196   Selfish people avoid responsibility, sacrifice, and situations in which they might tire themselves out. They wish to create their own heaven here on earth, but they risk losing the heaven that lasts for all eternity.

197   A person of character regards everyone in the world as a brother or sister and looks upon their work as his or her own. The selfish person regards everyone as rungs of a ladder to be used for his or her own advancement.

Such a person knows only "my" work and "my" possessions.

198   To exploit people in order to advance your own interests is unworthy of a leader. You will be a worthy leader if you do not distance yourself from people, but mingle with them and risk yourself for their sake.

199   Do not confuse cowardice with prudence. It is because so many people have this kind of "wisdom" that darkness prevails in so many situations.

200   A person of character is not self-satisfied. Self-satisfaction is like a curtain that separates one from God, from others, and from everything else — it leads to self-sufficiency.

201   The great-hearted person is not boastful, but possesses a spirit of self-sacrifice. This person is like a lump of sugar or grain of salt which, when dissolved, adds flavor to food.

202   The great-hearted person is straightforward and neither pries into the affairs of others nor deals with them in a devious manner.

203   A person of character does not go about interfering in people's business and knows his or her limitations.

204   Know when to keep quiet. Too much gossip, without thought of the consequences, spreads disharmony. Idle words undermine charity.

205   Do not be inquisitive, but concentrate on knowing yourself more fully.

206   The habit of making critical comments is one of the biggest obstacles to growth in the spiritual life. Blaming others irritates them and cultivates bitterness in your own heart.

207   Never use failure, trials, or sufferings as an occasion to blame others.

208   "Laissez-faire" is a word in the dictionary of cowards — those lazy people who do not wish to struggle and have already accepted defeat.

209   Avoid false humility. It is necessary to be ambitious in the search of knowledge, in the desire to act and to take risks, but all of this for God and for the Church.

210   Refrain from violent arguments that lead to a loss of perspective. Passion can be a dark cloud that blocks out God's light.

211   Friction among people is a normal part of life. A society without friction exists only in heaven. By means of friction a stone can become smoother, rounder, cleaner, and more beautiful.

212   Do not be contaminated by superficiality. This disease causes the gradual death of the will. Its symptoms are a frequent change of opinion and of activity. To

avoid it, do not accumulate a stockpile of projects which are never carried out.

213   The superficial person is like a puppet that dances around but is ineffective and useless. You must attend to your projects today and not wait for tomorrow to act.

214   God did not create us to be like a flock of sheep; he created us to lead others. To lead means to urge and encourage and to carry others along with us.

215   All the small things you do are very important; do not despise them. If you progress in small things, you will train your will to be rock-solid and you will master yourself.

216   When you wish to say something, consider how you will say it. Charity and politeness will help your message to be better received. The same message delivered in two different ways by two people with different mindsets produces two different results.

217   Do not browbeat the person who has done something wrong. Wait patiently; you will achieve more by speaking gently and with good will than by abuse. By so acting and controlling your temper, you will make your point.

218   Resolve to do what has to be done without fear or hesitation. Be courageous and full of hope; trust in God and in your own courage!

219   When you are confronted with obstacles, stand as firm as a rock. The grace of God will not be lacking. If you must curtail your activities for a time, it is unimportant. After all, the work you do is God's more than your own.

220   Time and energy belong to God. Why do you squander them on obstacles along the way? The ocean is full of waves, yet a boat continues to glide over the water and ignore the waves.

221   Be calm and self-possessed. Why do you allow yourself to become so agitated and angry? Such an attitude irritates those around you and makes you unhappy as well. And of what use is it when you are left with regrets after the incident has passed?

222   Do not say, "I was made like this; I cannot change." No, we are talking about your faults and imperfections. As a true child of God, you must be mature and deliberately continuing in these faults and imperfections prevents you from becoming such a person.

223   Turn your back on those small-minded people who whisper in your ear, "You are mad to put up with such a miserable life!" Remember how Jesus dismissed Peter: "Get behind me, Satan! You are an occasion of sin for me — you are setting your thoughts not on divine things but on human things" (Mt 16:23).

224   You should strive to acquire the ability of being able to refuse, and of knowing how to say "No."

225   Do not be particular as to where you live or work. Open wide your heart so that every person may have a place there, otherwise you will be Christian in name but not in reality.

226   Illumine your life with the virtues of faith and charity. Set fire to the world with the flame God has placed in your heart.

227   Act in such a way that your thoughts, words, and deeds will cause others to remark: "This is a person steeped in one book, the Gospel, and inspired by one ideal, the life of Jesus Christ."

228   Be serious and constant. Your exterior demeanor should reflect your interior life — that is, your peace of soul and self-control — rather than childish fear.

229   When Margaret Mary Alacoque entered the convent, she did not like cheese. Not wanting to be different than the others, she struggled at meals for seven long years: "I must eat cheese — I can't eat it — I must eat it!" Eventually she triumphed over herself and was able to eat it. Such is the fortitude of the saints!

CHAPTER 11

The Presence of God

If God is present, your life
will be lonely no longer.

230   Put your hand over your heart often and tell yourself: "God is living with me and in me." Little by little, God will give you a taste of that happiness which his presence brings.

231   When we teach children to answer the question: "Where is God?" with, "God is in heaven," there is something missing. We should add, "God is living in me." This answer is far more accurate and will bring them into a closer relationship with God, and greater happiness.

232   Thousands of patients in the House of Saint Joseph of Cottolengo have a special expression on their faces

for, from time to time, a gentle voice is heard repeating over the public address system: "God is here in our house."

233 The pealing of a bell or the spire of a church is a reminder that Jesus is in a tabernacle nearby. Then raise your heart toward that place to worship and love God.

234 God's presence to you is not just a pious idea; it is a reality. God our Father is at your side with all his power and love. He is the Father who persuades you, who counsels you, who calls you, who admonishes you, who forgives you, and who loves you always.

235 Jesus is everything to you; he is the object of all your desires, the reason behind all your decisions, the power beneath all your emotions, and the model of all your actions.

236 Think for a moment of the presence of a very loving and inspiring person, or of a gentle, caring mother — even of a distinguished guest who affirms you, makes you feel grateful and self-confident. But all that love, kindness, and honor are nothing when compared with that which God's presence offers you. God's presence exceeds all others to such an unfathomable degree that a million times the distance between earth and heaven would not begin to express its infinite superiority.

237 Why do some Christians complain that they are lonely? Where is their Christ?

238　　Consider the greeting of the angel: "Hail, full of grace, the Lord is with you!" (Lk 1:28), and the greeting of the Church: "The Lord be with you." Aren't these greetings full of profound significance and capable of changing your life?

239　　In your relationship with God, your conscience is sufficient, but with other people, you also need wisdom because their eyes do not see your conscience.

240　　Ask Mary to lead you to Jesus and you will know what it is to live by his side.

241　　The reality of the presence of God by your side is not just a question of feelings. God takes complete possession of you, leading, loving, and consoling you.

242　　Live at God's side and you will become a saint, since heaven is nothing other than the presence of God.

243　　Speak frequently to Mary, the beloved Mother of God. This is most pleasing to God, who is present in your heart.

244　　Since the Blessed Trinity is living in you, you are the temple of God. You are also a holocaust, a word of unending praise, a flower of great beauty offered up to God.

245　　Why are you so eager to build churches of wood and stone for God and yet are unwilling to make your soul a temple of God?

246   Do not be concerned about whether you live in a beautiful mansion or a simple hut, so long as you make your home an abode of love. Then it will become heaven, because God will be there.

CHAPTER 12

The Church

One Body: The Church.
One Leader: The Holy Father.
One Hope: "So that all may be one" (Jn 17:21).

247 Whenever anyone expressed their concern to Pope Paul VI about his sufferings or the fatigue of his labors, he would always reply: "For the Church! For the Church!" You should try to live and respond in a similar fashion.

248 A person who really loves the Church does not seek to destroy it.

249 "You are Peter, and on this rock I will build my church, and the gates of hell will not prevail against it" (Mt 16:18). Twenty centuries have passed since Jesus uttered these words to Peter. There have been so many ups and downs, so many crises, attacks from within and without. There have been many periods when the

Church was in desperate straits. Yet the Church still stands firm because it is the Church of God and not a mere human institution.

250   "We believe in one, holy, catholic, and apostolic Church" *(Nicene Creed)*. We have but one faith; we know the same happiness; we share a like determination!

251   Do not be surprised when people seek to destroy the Church. They seek to kill Christ again, but since they cannot do so, they seek to destroy the Church which is the Body of Christ.

252   There are many people who criticize the organization of the Roman Curia. I would agree with them that the Roman Curia is not perfect, but I would ask them whether their own government is any better. Besides, one must distinguish between the Curia, which is only a human organ of the Church, and the Church itself, the Body of Christ.

253   Love the Church. Obey the Church. Be loyal to the Church. Pray for the Church.

254   Some people have a distorted idea of the Church. They criticize the Curia as being too slow to move. They find church buildings too ornate or not ornate enough, ceremonies too elaborate or not elaborate enough. But the Curia, church buildings, and ceremonies are not the Church. Rather, the Church is the entire people of God advancing toward the kingdom of heaven.

255   It is necessary to distinguish between questions of theology and of history. The pope may not necessarily be the most capable person in the Church, but he is the one chosen by God to exercise authority over the Church in his name. He is the one you must obey because it is to him that God "has entrusted the keys of the kingdom of heaven" (cf. Mt 16:19).

256   Liturgical prayer is not aimed only at our personal salvation or liberation. Liturgical prayer unites us with the entire People of God throughout the world because it unites us with Christ our Head, and with his Vicar on earth, the Holy Father. Humanity is set free by the continued memorial of the death and resurrection of Christ. Without this unity, we would be like a branch cut off from the vine: we would be Catholic in name only.

257   Do not say that the Church *has* been renewed, but rather that the Church *is being* continuously renewed.

258   The Church was born on the cross and it grows by continuing the passion of Jesus until the end of time. If you put your trust in money, in diplomacy, in power, influence, or campaigns of any kind, you will be very sadly misled.

259   You say that you would never turn against the Church, but you do not hesitate to oppose the representatives of the Church. If this is how you think, you are playing games!

260   You attack structures, but then you insist upon having organizations of various kinds, appointing various persons, creating committees and sub-committees, setting up offices.... You are like a group of people that criticizes the foolish practice of organizations that abbreviate their names, such as UNO, UNESCO, etc., and then sets up a society called "AWA" (Association Without Abbreviations), creating one more organization!

261   There are various kinds of believers: there are those who merely make use of the Church, there are those who are Catholic in name only, there are the opportunists, and there are the honorary Catholics who are looking for status. The Lord desires those who accept him unconditionally: "They left everything and followed him" (Lk 5:11).

262   Naturally, no one sets out to betray the Church simply for the sake of betraying it. Very often circumstances lead them to do so, especially these three: when they are caught up in financial or emotional problems; when their ambition is thwarted; when threatened with suffering of some kind, even death itself.

263   During the last two thousand years, the Church has been betrayed by apostles, popes, cardinals, bishops, priests, religious, and lay people in the extraordinary ways which Paul VI called "self-destruction." However, after each of these upheavals, the Church has renewed itself and become ever more fresh and brilliant

and strong. The Church continues to live the mystery of the passion and resurrection.

264   Within the Church today, there is much imperfection and many instances of scandal. And yet, the Church enjoys God's promise; the Church is a continuous miracle.

265   Be ready to sacrifice for the Church and through the Church.

266   "Whoever hears you, hears me, and whoever rejects you, rejects me. And whoever rejects me, rejects the One Who sent me" (Lk 10:16). Throughout your life keep the following advice firmly impressed on your heart. Always respect those people who represent the Church, the sacraments of the Church, the teachings of the Church, and the liturgy of the Church.

267   Everyone in the Church is called, indeed has the duty, to become holy. If you are not leading a holy life, you should not presume to reform the Church. "I want you to know that no one speaking under the influence of God's Spirit can say, 'Cursed be Jesus!' and no one can say, 'Jesus is Lord!' except under the influence of the Holy Spirit" (1 Cor 12:3).

268   You believe in the one Church that our Lord Jesus Christ established and you suffer because of the imperfections you see on the human face of the Church. But you share the responsibility for those imperfections.

You must strive to eradicate them and to carry out the will of God in the Church.

269   Before you criticize the Church as being removed from social reality, read the documents and encyclicals of the popes. You will be surprised to discover that they have dealt with every problem with deep insight. You will see just how radical and advanced were their policies of renewal, drawn from the Scriptures, the grace of God, and tradition. As Pope Pius XII once said, if we put into practice even a little of the popes' teachings, the Church and the world would be transformed.

270   The Church belongs to young and old, intellectuals and workers, to poor and rich alike. The Church belongs to those races of yellow, black, and white skin; it belongs to women as well as men. The Church is universal and it accepts all people without distinction. Discrimination and division have no place in the Church.

CHAPTER 13

Faith

Light up the world with the flame of faith.

271   As you travel along the Road of Hope, you will need a light to show you the way during times of darkness and difficulties. That light is your faith, which the Church passed on to you on the day of your baptism.

272   If you are faced with the most desired of promises or the most fearful of threats, you must remind yourself: "I am a child of the Church, I am a descendant of the saints, I follow the faith which guides me."

273   If you wish to hold firmly to your faith, then choose the Road of Hope which was followed by Christ's disciples, not the road to death offered by "the world."

274   Many people say, "I have the faith; I still have the faith." Perhaps this is true, but their daily lives are often at variance with the faith they profess. Few people live in complete accord with faith.

275   An examination of your actions and reactions will suffice to indicate whether yours is a living, vibrant faith, or simply a label.

276   The Lord lays down very easy conditions for our faith to accomplish great things: "If you have faith like a grain of mustard seed you'll say to this mountain, 'Move from here to there!' and it will move, and nothing will be impossible for you" (Mt 17:21). Why? Because it is God who performs the action and not ourselves.

277   We do not believe in a God who is far away and vague, but we believe with the faith of Peter: "You are the Messiah, the Son of the Living God!" (Mt 16:16), and with the faith of John: "Whoever does not love does not know God, because God is love" (1 Jn 4:8).

278   If you have strong faith, you can do anything. Each time the Lord performs a miracle in the Gospels, he says: "Your faith has healed you."

279   In the Gospels the apostles humbly related their own weakness of faith so that we may believe more strongly.

280   Don't be satisfied with a theoretical and formal faith. Rather let your faith be living, genuine, loving, and loyal.

281   There is no peace compared with the confidence which comes from living as a member of the Church. In

the heart of the Church mental anxiety is calmed and the soul is filled with hope.

282 Like the apostles, pray sincerely: "Lord, increase our faith!" (Lk 17:5).

283 Faith is the unconditional acceptance of Jesus Christ the Lord, and the determination to live and die with him.

284 God is almighty and everlasting. If you believe in him you will do extraordinary things just as Jesus did. In fact, you will do even greater things, as he promised (cf. Jn 14:12).

285 Do not pretend in order to escape dangers and difficulties. Remember the example of Eleazar: "'Such pretense is not worthy of our time in life,' he said, 'for many of the young might suppose that Eleazar in his ninetieth year had gone over to an alien religion, and through my pretense, for the sake of living a brief moment longer, they would be led astray because of me, while I defile and disgrace my old age'" (2 Mac 6:24–25).

286 Even though you are not being forced to deny the Lord, you may be under pressure to act in opposition to his teaching in the mistaken hope of preserving your faith. But don't be deceived — faith that fears death, suffering, or hardships surely dies.

287 Have the courage to live the life of faith every day, just as the martyrs courageously held firmly to their faith.

288   As a follower of Christ, believe above all that you have been redeemed, forgiven, and are infinitely loved by God. The Lord is not a Savior who forces us to love and reverence him; rather he is the Savior who invites us to love him without reservation.

289   God is supreme not only because he is almighty, but especially because he is all-loving.

290   The redemption of humanity should not be thought of in terms of action, but in terms of mystery — the mystery of the death and resurrection of our Lord Jesus Christ.

CHAPTER 14

The Apostle

*The apostle makes present again
the life of Jesus.*

291   To be an apostle means to be like the apostles, so if you wish to be an apostle, you must reflect on and grow to understand the Acts of the Apostles.

292   The faithful of the early Church commonly described an apostle as a person with Christ in his or her heart, demeanor, speech, actions, and even body. In a word, an apostle is a person filled with Christ and who spends his or her life transmitting Christ to others.

293   Apostolic work involves the sanctification of the milieu in which you are present. The worker is an apostle of workers, the student is an apostle of students, and the soldier is an apostle of soldiers.

294   "Whoever holds out till the end, they will be saved" (Mt 10:22), so let us pray and support one another.

295   Of themselves, good works do not make the apostle; a real apostle performs good works because they are part of Christ's mission.

296   We live in a new period of time — it has new needs and demands new methods in the apostolate. However, Christ said: "Behold, I will be with you all the days until the end of the age" (Mt 28:20). He is still with the Church and he continues to give the Church a new Pentecost.

297   Work with all your heart and soul, but be ready to share with everyone and to cooperate with those who may be less capable than yourself. Do not control everything as if nothing would get done without you.

298   There are things that you yearn to do, but you cannot. Often these heartfelt desires are more pleasing to God, and more meritorious, than all the results which give *you* satisfaction rather than God.

299   Do not be discouraged by difficulties. Ask yourself, "Is this God's work or mine? Is God doing this or am I?"

300   Before you complain about this person or that person, ask yourself, "Is my own salt still full to the taste? Is my own lamp still bright?"

301   It is necessary to be selective, but do not criticize, distrust, or despise others. The apostles Jesus chose to build the Church were also filled with imperfections. He only required that they be childlike and follow him loyally.

302   To the degree that your ego grows will your apostolic work be a failure. The more you allow your ego to die, so much the more will your apostolic work flourish (cf. Jn 3:30).

303   Be ready to sacrifice comforts which you see as unbecoming for the authentic apostle. Do not create "needs" that are not truly necessities.

304   Do not be a person who talks much but does little. Do not give great attention to action but little attention to prayer. Do not accept freely but give sparingly. Do not be easy on yourself but strict toward others.

305   The light of your apostolic activity must shine for others until the darkness is overcome and the world is totally immersed in the light of Christ. Be an apostle to apostles.

306   No one is the sole representative of God in ministry. When the apostles complained to the Lord, "Teacher, we saw someone driving out demons in your name and we tried to stop him, because he was not following us" (Mk 9:38), the Lord told them, "Whoever is not against us is for us" (Mk 9:39).

307   You are surprised or annoyed when others do not follow your style. It is true that there must be unity, but

there are many facets to this unity. Paul tells us: "some proclaim Christ out of jealousy and contentiousness, but others proclaim him out of good will.... What does it matter? The important thing is that one way or another Christ is proclaimed" (Phil 1:15, 18).

308   Just as no two stars in the heavens are alike, no two saints are alike. Yet the saints are all alike in one aspect: they reflect the life of Jesus.

309   In any apostolic work, it is of the utmost importance to choose and train zealous co-workers. One leader was heard to say, "Give me 300 brave soldiers and I will rule until death." Jesus chose only twelve and his rule will last till the end of the world.

310   There is no need for any special rank or position to do the work of an apostle. Do not feel uncomfortable on account of your position or that of others. Are you working for God or for status? "You will, indeed, drink my cup, but as for sitting at my right hand or left, that is not mine to give — it is for those for whom it has been prepared by my Father" (Mt 20:23).

311   The apostle may have one position today and another tomorrow, but he or she does not feel any loss whatsoever. The apostle is conscious of one call: "The Son of Man came, not to be served, but to serve, and to give his life as a ransom for many" (Mt 20:28).

312   You experience sadness because of the loss of a position, or because you are not put in the right posi-

tion. Why do you think in business terms, where one must be so calculating?

313   To accept the responsibility of an apostle means to possess the readiness to accept martyrdom — with the love and perseverance of Peter and John — whenever, however, and at whoever's hands it is suffered. "So the apostles left the Sanhedrin, rejoicing that they had been considered worthy to be dishonored for the sake of the name" (Acts 5:41).

314   The most dangerous enemy of apostolic work is the enemy within. It was an apostle who betrayed the Lord.

315   The most harmful enemy of your apostolic life is not an external enemy, your adversary, but an internal enemy. You could become a double agent, attempting to work for both sides: God's and the devil's.

316   An apostle respects higher authority even when he or she could show the authority that a mandate is unsuitable. In the presence of others, an apostle always treats a superior with respect. Disobedience and duplicity are inexcusable.

317   If you display an air of self-satisfaction, you will repel others and no one will believe that you do things under the guidance of the Holy Spirit.

318   If you do battle with the enemy on all sides and have not charity, all your efforts will be useless. This would be like your buying a set of colored lights and stringing them across a village that has no electricity. The night comes and it is pitch black. Then the villagers learn the truth: your set of lights may decorate, but cannot light up the village.

319   If you should be insulted, persecuted, or driven out of one town to another, this is a sign that God loves you and that he has chosen you to be a true apostle. "If you had been of the world the world would have loved its own, but because you are not of the world, but instead I chose you from the world, therefore, the world hates you. Remember the word I spoke to you, 'A servant isn't greater than his lord.' If they persecuted me, they will also persecute you, if they kept my word, they will keep yours as well" (Jn 15:19–20).

320   Apostolic work is aimed at bringing others into the Church, not at establishing a partisan or national church. Such attempts, though not definitely schismatic, are a great hindrance to the work of the Church.

321   An apostle who suffers, even though he or she does not preach or perform great works, can quietly sacrifice him or herself for the salvation of others. Thus, while Jesus was in agony as he hung dying on the cross, Mary was suffering an agony of soul at the foot of the cross.

322   There are many ways of being an apostle.
       An apostle of sacrifice: Sacrifice is like a grain of rice. Buried in a field, it gives birth to millions of grains to feed humanity.

An apostle of witness: Witness affects others. Empty resolutions, however eloquent and promising they seem, convince no one. Solid evidence is more convincing. If you have photographs of a person, or a recording of that person's voice, people are readily impressed. But if that person is actually present in flesh and bones, or better, if that person's entire family or community are all loving according to the same ideal, what a great, persuasive force that witness would have!

323   An apostle of personal contact: "Were not our hearts burning within us while he spoke to us on the road, as he opened up the Scriptures to us?" (Lk 24:32). Every contact is an apostolic encounter.

324   An apostle of counseling others: There are also those who exercise their apostolate by counseling, thus bringing hope to nearly shattered lives. They help those in crisis by opening up horizons that allow others to realize their own potential and to clearly perceive the call of faith. If there were more people like those apostles, there would be fewer stories in the news about people committing suicide.

325   An apostle at the dining table: A meal is an every-day event, but Jesus' dining at the houses of Mary and Martha, of Simon, and of Zacchaeus is no different from his dining with us. His presence is salvific: "Today salvation has come to this house" (Lk 19:9).

326   An apostle of the pen: Why do you think that correspondence is not an apostle's work? When Paul was in prison he had no printing press, yet he still wrote letters to the Christian communities. These were copied and passed on to other communities. In this way Paul held firmly to and developed the faith of the early Church.

327   Women are very capable apostles. Look at Mary and Salome who followed and helped the Lord. Paul's letters also reflect an esteem for women, for example: "Greet Tryphaena and Tryphosa, laborers in the Lord" (Rom 16:12).

328   From the earliest times, young children who were filled with great courage became apostles; Tarcisius brought the Lord to many people. Recall Jesus' words: "Let the children come to me! Do not stop them!" (Mk 10:14).

329   The contemporary struggle of women for recognition in the Church should not be necessary. The apostles gave women recognized roles in the work of the early Church. Paul writes: "I commend to you our sister Phoebe, a deacon in the church at Cenchreae. Receive her in the Lord in a manner worthy of the saints and help her with anything she may need from you, for she has been a benefactor to many people, including myself. Greet Prisca and Aquila, my co-workers in Christ Jesus. They risked their own necks to save my life, and

not only I but also the Gentile churches thank them"
(Rom 16:1–4).

330   Do not have doubts regarding your call, or that of
others, to be apostles: whether a fisherman like Peter or
a tax collector like Matthew, everyone can be an
apostle. "Follow me, and I will make you fish for
people!" (Mt 4:19). You cannot do this yourself; it is
the work of the Lord.

331   Prepare your heart to receive and carry out all of the
Church's plans for evangelization.

332   In the past, people would risk their lives to find
precious spices or a gold mine. Today, countries will
destroy each other to obtain petroleum, iron, copper,
phosphate, or uranium. But, when it concerns people's
spiritual lives, no one is eager to search them out.

333   If one said that the laity have the charism of the
Holy Spirit, some people would not take it seriously. If
one stated that the laity are priests, prophets, kings,
those same people would not believe it. How many of
the laity understand the fact that they have been called
by God and that God needs them? How many are proud
and grateful for having been made children of God
through baptism and witnesses by confirmation?

334   This is the age of the laity. As long as we fail to
mobilize the strength and talents of the People of God,
to make them aware of and active in their apostolic

roles, there will remain a large strata of society that waits to be imbued with the Gospel.

335   The secret of the apostolate in our time is the lay apostle.

336   Just as seminary training is essential for the priest, an initial period of formation is absolutely necessary for every lay apostle.

337   A parish which invests in training just five genuine lay apostles would be assured of loyal service, even unto death, for thirty or forty years. How much potential we fail to discover and use for the kingdom of God!

338   Do not be too eager for large numbers. The example of the political cadre will convince you of this. Large numbers of people can be disparate and difficult to manage. On the political scene only one party cadre is required to stir up fervor and activate the masses as the soul, the mind, the very backbone of the people.

339   Let us look at secular institutes, for instance. They are new solutions for the problems of a new era. They are the special grace granted to our times to promote a lay spirituality. The popes foresaw this development decades before its appearance.

340   The role of the apostle in our time is to be in the midst of the world — not of the world, but for the world and making use of the things of the world.

341   As members of the Body of Christ, we are the mind that meditates, the eyes that look at the reality of the world, the ears that hear needs and requests, the shoulders that support, the arms that rescue, the feet that go to those who are suffering, the heart that brings compassion and love to those who are anxious, the mouth that speaks words of love and consolation. It is by its apostles that the Church is present in the world today.

342   People do not notice the humble presence and quiet activity of the apostle, but in the apostle's absence they immediately feel that their environment is empty and as cold as the grave. We take the salt in the sea, the light and the air for granted, but without them the world would not survive. We are scarcely aware of the forces of nature operating around us, but if they ceased, we would also be wiped out.

CHAPTER 15

The Eucharistic Celebration

*An eternity of preparation and
of thanksgiving alone suffice
to appreciate one Eucharistic Celebration.*

343   The Eucharist shapes Christians; Christians shape the Eucharist. The Eucharist shapes the Church; the Church shapes the Eucharist.

344   Non-Catholics think it is strange: they ask, "If day after day the priest does the same things at Mass, why do Catholics continue gathering together to celebrate?" What they say is partly correct; whoever celebrates and wherever it is celebrated, the Eucharistic Celebration is the one sacrifice of Calvary. But it is the power of mystery that draws people, for it is Jesus himself who offers the sacrifice.

345 Some people contend that only by going to Mass when they feel fervent are they being sincere with God. This is not true; in fact, such people go to Mass for their own self-satisfaction.

346 If you appreciate the value of the Eucharistic Celebration you will participate in it no matter how far away or difficult it is. The greater the sacrifice involved, the more evident is your love of God.

347 Have you ever met someone who became materially deprived simply because he spent too much time in Church?

348 People celebrate Eucharist together, but their sentiments can be vastly different. So it was at the foot of the cross, as a study of those who stood there shows.

349 If you wonder by what means you can most please God, the answer is: celebrate the Eucharist. There is no prayer, no meeting, no ceremony that is comparable to the prayer and sacrifice of our Lord on the cross.

350 Holy people are those who continue to live the Eucharistic Celebration throughout the day.

351 We find chatting for hours with a friend pleasant. When it comes to eating and drinking, the more time we spend dining, the more we enjoy it. And some find gambling the night away an exciting pastime. Why then are we in such a hurry when we go to Church?

352   "A lukewarm priest in a cathedral attracts no one, but a holy priest in a poor, shabby chapel in some remote part of the world attracts crowds" (Father Chevrier).

353   A family that loves the Eucharist will be a holy family.

354   "An eternity of reparation and an eternity of thanksgiving alone suffice to appreciate one holy Mass" (John Mary Vianney).

355   The priest celebrates the Eucharist in union with the Lord; when he distributes Holy Communion he gives himself in union with the Lord as food for all, thus signifying that he is totally available to others at all times.

356   The whole of the Lord's life was directed toward Calvary. The whole of our life should be oriented toward the Eucharistic Celebration.

357   Each time you celebrate Eucharist, you have the opportunity to stretch out your hands and nail yourself to the cross with Jesus, to drink his bitter chalice to the dregs. There is no place for mere spectators at Eucharist.

358   I like the expression, "to offer Mass." All are united in Christ in the Eucharist and thus share in his eternal offering.

359   Do you wish to give glory to God? To give thanks to God? To pray to God? Do you wish to love God? Do

you wish humanity to be saved? Then celebrate the
Holy Eucharist. It was through his sacrifice on Calvary
that our Lord accomplished all of this.

360   An oil lamp cannot give light if it has no oil. A car
cannot run on an empty gas tank. An apostle will degen-
erate without receiving the Eucharist: "Unless you eat
the flesh of the Son of Man and drink his blood, you do
not have life within you" (Jn 6:53).

361   As the sun shines brightly and sheds its light, so the
Eucharist is the light and the source from which ema-
nate spiritual life and harmony among nations. "But the
bread that I will give for the life of the world is my
flesh" (Jn 6:51).

362   Through the Blessed Eucharist we are united in the
Body of Christ. To celebrate the Eucharist without love
is a contradiction, an anomaly.

363   If you lack everything or have lost everything, but
still have the Blessed Sacrament, you actually still have
everything, because you have the Lord of heaven
present here on earth.

364   If you are all alone in some remote place or in the
darkness of a prison, turn your mind toward the altars of
the world where our Lord Jesus Christ is offering his
sacrifice. Unite yourself to the Eucharistic sacrifice.
Then your heart will be filled to overflowing with consolation and courage.

365   The Eucharistic Celebration and the reception of Holy Communion are inexhaustible subjects for meditation. How can you complain of being unmoved by them?

366   The mere "Sunday Catholic" will never reform today's materialistic world. To live the Eucharist is the secret of bringing God to the world and of leading the world to God.

367   Jesus began a revolution on the cross and your "revolution" must begin at the table in order to be an extension of his. Thus will humanity be renewed.

368   As the drop of water put into the chalice mingles with the wine, so your life should become one with Christ's.

369   Your whole life should proclaim the death of the Lord and witness to his resurrection.

370   Jesus is the head and he offers the Eucharist only in communion with his Body, the Church. The eucharistic prayer declares that the offering is made by the people "together with the pope and bishop." Only within this unity has the Eucharist true meaning as an acceptable sacrifice.

371   The Eucharist renders the Church present to me and allows me to live with the Church. I listen to the words of our Divine Savior, the prophets, and the apostles. I

am united with Mary, the saints, the holy souls and with
the Holy Father, with my bishop, the hierarchy, the
clergy, the religious, the entire People of God, in order
that through, with, and in Jesus Christ I may offer all
glory and honor to the Holy Trinity in expectation of
the glorious coming of our Lord. How great is the happiness and the hope I receive in the Eucharist!

372   My whole life can be a continuous Eucharistic celebration: at times a penitential rite, at other times praying the "Our Father" or joyfully chanting "glory to
God" or singing "alleluia." Whatever the circumstances, it is always an offering, a summons to prayer, a
proclamation of my faith in one God, united with all
people through the action of the Holy Spirit and in
communion with the Church throughout the world.

373   If you wish to strengthen your faith you must nourish yourself with the blessed Eucharist, which is the
"Mystery of Faith" and fortifies faith.

374   A seminarian is nourished with the Eucharist so that
he may become a golden grain of wheat that dies and is
crushed to become the bread of Christ's body given as
food for the People of God.

375   The dedicated seminarian or priest understands that
every day is a solemnity when the Eucharist is celebrated. Every day demands the solemnity of a sung
Mass that is celebrated with ever growing fervor —
right up to the last.

376   Each time you distribute the Eucharist, remind yourself of the reality that together with Christ you are giving your whole life: your time, your energy, your talents, and your possessions. In a word, with the Body and Blood of the Lord, you give your own flesh and blood to be the nourishment of each and every person without distinction.

377   Unite yourself to Jesus every day. Be ever more prepared to be "given" for your brothers and sisters, to shed your own blood if necessary so that "sins may be forgiven" (cf. Mt 26:28).

378   Every day at the words of consecration, with all your heart and soul, renew "the new and everlasting covenant" between Jesus Christ and yourself by the mingling of your blood with his.

379   The Eucharist gives the mind some understanding both of the mysteries of the kingdom of heaven hereafter and of the union of the People of God in this mystery. Our faith depends upon our belief in the mystery of the kingdom of heaven. The faith of a person who lives without the Eucharist would not survive for long.

380   The priesthood is centered on an ardent desire for the Eucharistic Celebration. It should be the focal point of your thoughts and the motivation of your actions. Then you will be able to say truly: "With what longing have I longed to eat this Passover with you" (Lk 22:15).

381   White, green, red, violet…the vestments may vary in color, but there is only one Eucharist in which you commemorate many events — joy, hope, martyrdom, mourning. Whenever or wherever you celebrate Eucharist, you do so "through him, with him, and in him."

382   Whenever you wear your clerical clothes, symbolic of the charity within you, you witness to the presence of God in the world. But have no fear, for even if you change your external appearance, people will recognize you as one of Christ's disciples if you love your neighbor (cf. Jn 13:35). On the other hand, if you do not have true love, or if your disposition is bad, however skillfully you may present yourself, people will not be convinced by your witness.

383   The Lord said, "For where two or three are gathered in my name, I am there among them" (Mt 18:20), and "Do this in remembrance of me" (1 Cor 11:24). Avoid the two extremes — anxiety that there is no place for the Lord to live and nettling criticism of those who work at building houses for God. Instead, rejoice! God does not lay down any material conditions. Such conditions are the invention of narrow-minded human beings.

384   When people no longer respect you as a priest or as a religious and you begin to experience greater austerity, more difficulties and privations because of your calling, rejoice and be glad! Never before has the image of God been so clearly revealed in you. Have confi-

dence, because when you are hung on the cross with Jesus, you will draw all things there to him (cf. Jn 12:32).

385   Do not think that your religious life has lost its meaning because you are not permitted to live in community, because you can no longer perform works of charity by educating or assisting those in need. What did Jesus do on the cross? What does Jesus do in the tabernacle? The Lord is present — praying and sacrificing. Can you see what meaning there is here for you? It was at the very moment that Christ died on the cross that he redeemed humanity.

386   If every means — schools, radio, television, public addresses, churches — are closed to you, do not bemoan the fact that you lack the means to bring Jesus to the world. Rest assured that while you seem to be deprived of everything, nothing is indispensable for God's work. You can follow the example of Mary everywhere in order to make God present. Remember Mary, our Mother!

387   The Church instructs us to celebrate the ceremony of religious profession during the Eucharistic Celebration in order to remind the religious that he or she offers God his or her life in union with the sacrifice on the altar. During every Eucharist, renew your vows with all your heart and with all the meaning of a "new and everlasting covenant."

388   Should all the churches on the face of the earth be
destroyed, we would still have the Eucharist wherever
there would still be a priest. Should every priest be
wiped out, wherever two or three would gather together
in our Lord's name, he would be there in the midst of
them (cf. Mt 18:20).

CHAPTER 16
Religious Obedience

A joyful acceptance indicates holiness.

389   Did you vow to obey your religious superiors or that your superiors obey you?

390   The person of weak character who loses control of his or her will is like a *mahout* (an elephant driver) that cannot control an elephant. The obedient person who has mastered his or her will is like a circus trainer who controls a tiger.

391   A disciplined army is a strong army. An obedient apostle will be a strong and courageous apostle.

392   You can tell how holy a person is by how readily and joyfully that person obeys.

393   "The world" may call such obedience folly, but it is God who asks you to obey for love of him. This is not folly, but heroic virtue.

394   Satan rebelled and he continuously incites rebellion with his motto: "I will not serve."

395   Our Divine Savior also led a revolution; millions upon millions have followed him and the motto: "Obedient, even unto death" (Phil 2:8).

396   Obedience allows for initiative, a search for greater understanding, and the presentation of a different point of view. But it also calls for careful listening, the acceptance of instruction, and attentive implementation.

397   There are some people who submit, but do not practice obedience. Others carry out instructions, but do not resign their own judgment. Still others submit and carry out orders, but only because they find their superior agreeable. Finally, there are those who obey without reservation and completely for love of God.

398   If your superior asks you to perform a difficult task, carry on as best you can and have trust. Is any task as difficult as conquering the world empty-handed as did the Lord? The apostles obeyed and they succeeded. Consider this miracle, which continues to this very day, and have confidence.

399   Do not expect your religious superior to be exemplary any more than you necessarily expect a doctor to be healthy. Exemplary conduct commands your respect, but in these circumstances you are simply following your own feelings rather than practicing virtue.

400   Even if you carried out some colossal tasks, but did not obey, you would not be pleasing to God. God values your heart; he has no need of your works. After all, he created the whole universe without your help.

401   The Church exists in the midst of society and it also needs a network of human organization. An act of disobedience inflicts a wound on the common life of the Church, just as one cell, if it is out of order, causes pain to the whole human body.

402   Purity means dying to being ruled by "the flesh," obedience means dying to being ruled by the will.

403   To carry out instructions while still obstinately rebelling against them is pride, not obedience.

404   Learn not to trust yourself too much, but to seek out and discuss things with experienced people. Have confidence that the hand of God arranges things through many people and many circumstances.

405   Obey in silence: the truth will set you free. Silence for five years, ten years, your whole life — silence in death. God knows you and that is sufficient. On the last day all of humanity will also know the truth.

406   "Obedience is greater than sacrifice," when the sacrifice consists of fruits, incense, animals, money, etc. When you obey, you sacrifice yourself; your will, your pride, become the holocaust (cf. Heb 10:5–7).

CHAPTER 17

The Spirit of Poverty

The Lord is your inheritance.
Is he not sufficient?

407   Your possessions will bury you if you carry them on your head or near your heart. Instead, your possessions will be your footstool if you stand on them.

408   "Be poor in the place where you live, in the clothes you wear, in the food you eat, in the things you use, in the work you do" (Father Chevrier).

409   The person who asks for little is content, because he or she considers anything to be sufficient. The person who asks for a great deal is extremely miserable because he or she always feels deprived.

410   When you look only at yourself and feel deprived, you can begin to think that you are the most miserable

person in the world. When you look at others, you will see how many people are worse off than yourself.

411   To have no possessions and to be avaricious for them is not the virtue of poverty. To have possessions and to be detached from them is to be truly poor in spirit.

412   Do not be open-handed with what belongs to others or stingy with your own possessions. Do not squander those things which belong to the whole community.

413   To be humble, to be considered the lowest in society, to be materially poor, or to suffer from an insufficient amount of food despite long and hard work, are only some instances of poverty. If you possess the spirit of poverty, you will be able to accept whatever circumstances you find yourself in.

414   Use your wealth with generosity, appreciate it with discernment, and be detached from it with fortitude, because it does not belong to you. God has entrusted it to you to share with the poor.

415   Quietly give to others your more convenient place or more profitable work. This is a sign of the genuine practice of the virtue of poverty.

416   You are the Lord's steward and are accountable for the possessions he has entrusted to you. If he has entrusted you with many things, then you have much to look after. If he has entrusted you with little, then you

have little to look after. If the Lord takes back what he has entrusted to you, be content.

417   Poverty that is envious, or is critical of others, or which harbors resentment are three kinds of poverty that are not evangelical poverty.

418   The world may not know that you are obedient and the world may not know that you are chaste, but the world can easily recognize your witness to poverty.

419   "O Lord, let me be poor like you." How often we make the opposite petition!

420   The expression, "The Church of the poor" does not mean that we would have people remain poor, but that we endeavor to improve people's lives in every respect.

421   What is the spirit of poverty? It is to possess as if not possessing; to sell as if not selling; to buy as if not buying; to act as if one had nothing at all and yet were master of everything — not demanding anything at all, but prepared to give everything.

422   Poverty does not mean being deprived of material possessions, which in themselves often bring misery and destitution. Poverty really means the proper attitude toward material possessions. Don't say: "It's *just* a cup of coffee or *just* a glass of wine!" Your enjoyment of these products might rest upon much toil, hardship, and even sacrifice on the part of those who produced them.

423   What is the first consideration regarding poverty? It is to work! When you understand the significance of the fatigue of daily labor you will experience a feeling of consolation. Yours will be the happiness Jesus spoke of in the Gospel: "Blessed is that servant who, when his Lord comes, he finds at work!" (Lk 12:43).

424   When, at the age of fifteen, Clare Offreduccio arrived at the monastery, she was asked by Francis of Assisi, "What are you seeking in coming here?" "I am looking for God," was her concise and clear response. That was her whole treasure and Clare became a saint. How many people know how to choose as she did?

CHAPTER 18
Chastity of Life

Prayer and sacrifice enrich the chaste heart.

425   "Blessed are the pure of heart, for they shall see God" (Mt 5:8). Priests and men and women religious are not the only people who must observe chastity. Everyone must do so according to his or her state in life. Living a chaste life does not mean being bound or restricted. Rather, it means greater freedom.

426   There are people who appear to be as pure as angels, but who are in fact demons of envy. How unhappy the community which meets with that kind of angel!

427   God grants the gift of chastity to humble souls who pray every day with a simple and sincere heart and who truly acknowledge their weaknesses.

428   The proud will sooner or later fall. They rely on their own strength rather than on God (cf. Rom 1:24).

429   The media call for the protection of, and struggle for, human and civil rights, but at the same time they can abuse their power by treating the human person as an object. Where are all the people who are struggling for the cause of human dignity? Where are all the organizations that are protecting humanity? Help should come from the very people who have a vested interest in the media and from their avid audience!

430   The devil can be driven away and "the world" can be kept at a distance, but "the flesh" you will carry until you die.

431   In order to live a chaste life, you must sacrifice. The alabaster-white lily, the fragrant cherry blossom, and the delicate peach blossom are beautiful because each takes root deep in the heart of the earth and holds out against the attacks of rain or tempest, while enduring the hands that prune them.

432   Chastity is meaningless without the virtue of charity. Do you practice your consecrated chastity because you are so selfish that you cannot tolerate anyone else? Or because you believe no one could possibly love you? Or is it because you desire to reserve your heart for loving God alone and for a more complete love of your neighbor? Only this last reason is a true motive.

433   There are many lay people who live exemplary lives of chastity. On observing their example, men and women religious should be struck with admiration and should be encouraged to make even greater efforts.

434   Many young people scoff at the idea of living a chaste life and regard the subject as old-fashioned. But when it comes to any unfaithfulness on the part of their own spouse, they become angry and jealous and even violent.

435   I have met many people from various walks of life and from different countries who were living happy single lives in the world. Their secret: "To live a life of prayer."

436   Priests and men and women religious give many reasons for departing from the celibate state, but many times they feel compelled to leave because they began an inappropriate emotional involvement and stopped praying.

437   Many saints overcame their difficulties. When will you make your decision?

438   Do not say that water could not put the fire out…it was because the fire was so intense and you used so little water!

439   "The flesh" is the enemy's commando lying in wait. If you do not strengthen your defenses with prayer, the sacraments, and sacrifices; if you do not wake up and watch, if you do not quell at once the slightest suggestion of rebellion each time it should appear, if you pamper the commando and cast aside your allies who are the saints and good companions, you will endure violent attacks and suffer a tragic defeat.

440　　Eating and drinking to excess is the way to open the door to the demon of impurity.

441　　How can a doctor effect a cure in a patient who insists he or she is not sick, refuses to be examined, and will not take the prescribed medication?

442　　Without chastity, your apostolate is a deception: "For where your treasure is, there will your heart be too" (Mt 6:21).

443　　Do not say, "I love them because they love me so much." You have to love yourself first. What would you accept in exchange for your soul?

444　　Do not make peace with lust any more than you would make peace with a disease, because both may be a matter of life or death.

445　　Your heart is not made of stone. Your heart is precious because it is made of flesh and capable of love. Courageously take hold of the holy cross with both hands and place it in your heart.

446　　Telling obscene stories, even for the sake of amusement, is not profitable. Never tell such stories. Experience shows that those who tell such stories often will eventually act them out. That is what psychological warfare is all about.

447   Do not engage in conversation with impurity, any more than you would stand by to watch the testing of an atomic bomb. Flight is the best strategy.

448   The saints were weak like yourself, some were even weaker, but thanks to that weakness, they became saints. They differ from you only in their determination.

449   "The flesh" is always very fragile and no matter what you wear, it is still there.

450   Your body is valuable because it was redeemed by the Precious Blood of Jesus, our Savior. Your body is the temple of the Holy Spirit and it will be glorious for all eternity. So do not put it up for sale!

451   The attractions offered by impurity are very alluring, and the defending attorney of "the flesh" pleads a strong case. Do not involve yourself in conversation with them. Realize that after a short moment of pleasure you will experience boredom, remorse, and loneliness.

452   Impurity fears only fasting and prayer. Have you practiced these yet?

453   The worst happens when you reject the advice of others and then award yourself pretentiously with a "Certificate of Chaste Conduct: Class A."

454   Never despise your neighbor who may have fallen while you have stood firm. If you have stood firm until now, it is thanks to the grace of God. Take care or tomorrow you may fall more seriously than your neighbor.

455   To disregard the power of your senses is to open the gate that allows the enemy into the fortress. David may have defeated Goliath, but he did not gain mastery over temptation.

456   Once you have risen from a fall, take hold of your weapons and fight with all your strength. An "open arms policy" — that is, surrendering your weapons and returning to the fold of temptation — is a very subtle enticement.

457   To suffer a defeat does not mean that the war has been completely lost. God can bring good out of everything, even sin.

458   With regard to my neighbors, I do not want to know or to remember their past. I wish only to think about their present, so that we may love and support one another.

459   The more you live a life of chastity, the more your willpower is strengthened, because it is trained in the midst of courageous struggles.

460   I have complete confidence in the Lord when I see how he forgave and defended sinners: "Let whoever is

without sin among you be the first to throw a stone at her," and "Neither do I condemn you. Go your way, and from now on sin no more" (Jn 8:7, 11). "Her sins, many as they are, have been forgiven, and so she has shown great love" (Lk 7:47).

461   People cannot easily understand chastity. Some think it is madness, some think it is too difficult, and some think it is not worthwhile. But in God's eyes it is of great value. A life of chastity can be realized only with God's help, and only God can give meaning to chastity.

CHAPTER 19

The Family

The family is a microcosm of the Church.

462   A person's happiness is not based on possessions or position, but on the love which he or she experiences through life.

463   For the preparation of priests we have seminaries, for the preparation of religious we have formation programs, for the preparation of teachers we have colleges, but for the preparation of parents we have nothing at all! This is indeed an enormous omission. There are some marriage preparation classes, but these still do not reach everyone. How many people will become victims of an adventure into which we seem to throw them so unprepared?

464   Reflect on the marriage feast of Cana (cf. Jn 2:1–10). In the beginning the guests were concerned with feasting and merry-making, but during the celebration the wine ran out and they were left only with water to

drink. Then, upon request, the Lord changed the water into wine, a wine that was more delicious than what had been served earlier. Remember that your own strength and resources are limited, and it is difficult to persevere in love. But God's grace is always available to assist you, to increase your resources abundantly, to intensify your love, and to secure happiness for your family. Make a place for the treasure of faith in your family.

465   While you are young, you go where you wish, but as an adult perhaps someone else, perhaps many others, perhaps many little hands will grasp your hand and take you where you would rather not go, where you would dare not go, where you would never have believed you would have the strength to go. But love is able to help you to do everything!

466   The married couple, both in regard to one another and in regard to their children, fully live out the Lord's love for everyone. Through this love the couple participates in and relives the mystery of the Redemption. The couple exercises this love completely and without limit in the same way that Jesus loves them and everyone.

467   The love of marriage has the power to stir the human heart to great courage, confidence, and generosity.

468   To look for change in one's partner without helping him or her through love to effect that change only creates frustration toward one's spouse. To expect that no change will be brought about by love is to underestimate him or her.

469   Love helps your spouse to grow and gives your spouse the means for growth. To force your spouse to change by making that change a prerequisite of your love completely removes the very means of bringing about change.

470   The unique way to secure a change in one's spouse is to accept him or her in love — just as when that love was new. Change is effected only when one knows and feels oneself to be loved.

471   Love is always full of expectation, not because you doubt your spouse's love, but because you feel the mutual responsibility to create things that are new, stimulating, and different — things that will surprise each other. This expectation is itself a source of happiness.

472   There is a regrettable human tendency to judge people according to their past. But there is also the human tendency, born of love, that understands how much a person can change for the better.

473   Love is not blind. Love sees the weakness of the beloved and tries to shoulder his or her burdens. Likewise love sees the abilities of the beloved and subtly encourages his or her potential.

474   If a person does not love the "flesh of his flesh and bone of his bones" and cannot bring happiness to this fundamental unit of society — upon which every other society is based — then how can such a person think of reforming the world?

475   In our time the Church has traced out a spirituality of marriage that allows us to see marriage as the means by which humanity develops and flourishes, and that it is a vocation to holiness.

476   Are you surprised to hear of "the vocation to be parents of a family"? People are mistaken when they restrict the idea of a vocation, that is, a calling to perfection, to the priest or religious alone. When, by means of the sacrament of Matrimony, two people solemnly swear to love one another in Christ for their entire lives, is this not a profession of faith, a profession of vows?

477   If the laity are to emphasize their particular mission in the world, then family life will be the most important and definite mission.

478   Reform the family in order to reform the Church.

479   You must shun the mistaken view of lay people as solitary, unattached individuals who do not belong to any community. You must put aside the negative habit of categorizing the laity as "those who are not priests or religious." Do not forget that the majority of the laity are people who live within families and who understand and live the sacrament of Matrimony.

480   It is truly regrettable that the civilized world's comprehension of the Catholic doctrine concerning marriage is limited to some of its prohibitions. From these the world does not gain the slightest inkling that Jesus came to redeem humanity through love, and that through the sacrament of Matrimony humanity is enriched in an extraordinary way. Therefore, study and present the beautiful and positive aspects of Catholic marriage.

481   In both the doctrinal and pastoral aspects of marriage we must strive to convince Catholic families of their own strength and help them to discover that they are not merely passive recipients of the teaching of the Church, but active participants in the apostolic work of marriage.

482   Mindful of their mission, many Catholic families put the human and supernatural forces of their conjugal love and of the sacrament of Matrimony under the direction and at the service of the Church with remarkable devotion.

483   To love your spouse is to act according to the will of God. When you realize this, you will understand that you can fulfill your vocation in the most ordinary circumstances of your life by perceiving God's call even in the most trifling activity. This is a revelation that will revolutionize your whole life.

484   The love between husband and wife is an image of the love of Christ for the Church (cf. Eph 5:31–32). In this mystery you will discover dignity, strength, and unity. The love that exists between a husband and wife is an extension of God's love. How uplifting and supportive is this love of the partners!

485   God has given you a loving spouse and beautiful children to help each other to become holy. What have you done with this gift?

486   Remember that you are responsible for your mutual growth toward maturity in the love of God, and that your vocation is to be together, and to become holy through this interdependence. Remember that the grace of the sacrament of Matrimony is unceasingly available to assist you in your vocation, and you are encouraged to fervently live the mystery of the death and resurrection in every aspect of your lives.

487   You must discover that you can and indeed have the responsibility to become holy in marriage and through marriage.

488   All the events of your lives as husband and wife, as parents; all your social responsibilities are so many opportunities for you to grow, to deny yourselves, and to advance along the road of true holiness.

489   The unity between husband and wife has to be absolutely complete: unity of body, love, mind, and spirit, through the presence of Christ. To love each other in God is very beautiful, and doing this for God's sake is even more beautiful; then, the whole family listens attentively to God and advances together toward greater intimacy with him.

490   The quiet moments spent side by side immersed in thought, praying spontaneously for one another and your children, exchanging intimacies concerning your spirituality and your apostolate are all a revelation and a profound, heartfelt happiness. May you experience the presence of God in your midst!

491   Having children is not only a response to the need to carry on the family lineage, but also a participation in the Body of Christ. The education of your children is the training of the faithful who will continue the worship of God the Father. Discover and admire the noble design which God has for your families.

492   You help your children to become children of God by teaching them to be active members of the Body of Christ. As parents your duty is to guide your children along the way in every respect and in every virtue.

493   The family is a microcosm of the Church, the Church in miniature. The Lord is present in his life, death, and resurrection in a mystical way in the members of the family. This reflection throws light on the meaning of the Catholic family and has the power to change it.

494   Contemplating the truth of the family as a microcosm of the Church makes us see clearly the primacy and the mission of the family in the following ways:

    1) it perpetuates the Church which Jesus Christ established in this world;
    2) the presence of God is realized in the family;
    3) the family witnesses to the presence of the Church in its day-to-day life;

4) the efforts of the family to be united to God help the entire Church to advance;

    5) the family strengthens the communion between God and each of its members.

495   Christ desired to build up his Mystical Body by means of the family. The Church may alter its methods of preaching, its various organizations, but the Church will always expand by means of families. The faith is spread through dynamic and healthy family units.

496   The education of children is a "school of perfection" for parents. Children possess a critical outlook and are sharp observers. They oblige you to carry out your role sincerely, and thereby help you to advance.

497   You can be assured that the life of the Catholic family is a very special way of life.

498   If we maintain that the world of labor should be sanctified by laborers, then we must believe that the Catholic family should be the primary apostle to other families.

499   People evaluate Catholic marriage according to the criterion of holiness in Catholic families.

500   Morning and night prayers in the family — or better put, times of family prayer — fulfill the duty of the family to become a community of Christians, one unit of the Church, according to the words of our Lord: "For where two or three are gathered in my name, I am there among them" (Mt 18:20).

501   The Catholic family is apostolic through its witness. You must show that you have been called to holiness and that you live a married life that is pleasing to God. Share with other families the grace and the happiness which God has bestowed on your family.

502   When every family becomes a source of light, the world will become one big family filled with light and hope.

503   The Catholic family is apostolic through hospitality. Open wide your homes and your hearts. What home does not have visitors? Hospitality is the most convenient and most natural way to bear witness to your love, your unity, your joy, and your openness to others. The art of hospitality can become the apostolate of hospitality. Live in such a way that anyone who visits your family desires to live like you.

504   When you sit side by side together in God's presence, it is a time of truth and of wonderful discovery. It is a dose of immortal medicine. The atmosphere of the family changes and many thorny problems are solved with mutual understanding. Where once a husband and wife might have lived together in a kind of "peaceful co-existence," now they are one in love, one in happiness, one in troubles, and one in prayer.

505   The first seminary, the first formation program, the first college is the Catholic family. No director, however talented or skilled, can replace parents. If this most fundamental unit breaks down, the future of the Church and of human society becomes shaky and risks collapse. On the day he turned fifty, Pope John XXIII wrote in a letter to his parents, "Dear Mom and Dad, today I have reached fifty years of age. God has given me many positions in the Church, I have been to many places, I have studied much, but no school has given me more instruction or has been more beneficial to me than that which I received when I sat on your laps."

CHAPTER 20

Humility

Learn a lesson from the Lord:
be meek and humble (cf. Mt 11:29).

506   If you truly understood the happiness that comes from being a child of God, humiliations would mean nothing to you, and likewise words of acclaim would add nothing to you.

507   If you knew yourself clearly, you would be amused by people's acclaim and not be surprised at contempt. You would also be surprised that you were not treated more harshly.

508   An apostle is humble and thanks God as Paul did: "For I am the least of the apostles, not even worthy to be called an apostle, because I persecuted God's church. But through the grace of God I am what I am, and the grace he gave me has not been without result" (1 Cor 15:9–10).

509   You are not practicing humility when you disparage yourself. Neither are you necessarily practicing humility when others disparage you. But, when others disparage you and you accept this situation for God's sake, then you are truly humble.

510   You will succeed in comprehending humility only through reflecting on the entire life of Jesus Christ. For love of each of us, the Son of God abased himself for thirty-three years and even accepted all the foolishness, ignorance, malice, and the rejection of his teachings from the people of his day.

511   In your pride, do you plunder God's grace and glory, trying to make them your property?

512   The humbler Mary became, the more glorious she was, because she saw more clearly the marvelous things God wrought in her soul. It is like light passing through a clear lightbulb on which there is no dust to hinder the passage of the light.

513   The person who lives in the presence of God cannot be proud. What is there to be proud of? Everything belongs to God.

514   Do not feign humility by refusing to do something, when in fact it is merely a pretext for avoiding the duty to commit yourself to God and perhaps risking some disgrace in the eyes of others.

515   Do not deny your talents or your successes. Rather, thank God that he uses you to do his work, just as an artist uses simple brushes to create a work of art.

516   Those who are truly humble will find peace and happiness, just as the Lord taught: "Learn from me, for I am gentle and humble of heart; and you will find rest for your souls" (Mt 11:29).

517   The humble person is like one who remains near to the ground. Instead, the proud person is like one who climbs up onto a high tower and stands at a height from which it is easy to tumble.

518   A determination to obey the Church is loyalty, and to choose tremendous sacrifice for the sake of one's mission is courage, not pride.

519   So long as you worship your ego you will be like a person who prays, "O Lord, believe in me; O Lord, hope in me."

520   Learning to accept your limitations is a very bitter trial. It is like being nailed to a cross: when the cross is broad the suffering is somewhat mitigated by the extra expanse, but when the cross is narrow your movement is restricted and your suffering will be much more terrible.

521   During his lifetime, Jesus especially loved the humble. He overlooked their sins and never mentioned them again. Such was the case for Peter, Matthew, and Zaccheus. Jesus invited himself to dine in their homes and accepted the reputation of being "a friend of tax collectors and sinners" (Lk 7:34).

522   Though it is impossible to avoid tension completely, it is possible to diminish it. In the first place, remember that God does not expect you to do everything; and secondly, God gives you the time and the means to carry out the work he has entrusted to you. If despite all your efforts and good will you cannot fulfill a task, then it is not God's will for you to complete it. Do not be tense or disappointed; remain calm!

CHAPTER 21

Prudence
in Speech

*Be circumspect like a seed
buried deep in the earth.*

523   Jesus Christ came into the world, and to carry out his mission according to the will of God the Father, he spent thirty of his thirty-three years in silence. He maintained his greatest silence during the days of his saving passion and death.

524   The more prudent you are, the fewer your regrets.

525   Do not expect that by talking a great deal, you will convince everyone to appreciate your point of view. In fact, the more you talk, the more you expose the flaws in your opinions. Then people will take the opposite position. The more you talk, the more you risk having your message distorted, and you will have to continually redefine and correct each of your statements.

526   When the Lord performed his miracles, he forbade that they be made public. After his transfiguration on Mount Tabor, he forbade the apostles even to speak about it (cf. Mt 17:9). This is an example to follow. Meditate on your apostolic ideal and carry it out faithfully with the help of the Holy Spirit. And remember that others will be ready to denigrate and oppose you if you are indiscreet.

527   Scripture gives us the examples of the Blessed Virgin Mary and of Judith's heroic deed performed in prudence. We also have the example of Delilah, who defeated the champion Samson because of his lack of prudence.

528   The seed which falls and is buried in the earth will yield flowers and fruit, but the seed which falls on the highway is snatched up by the birds of the air or crushed beneath the passing traffic and is wasted (cf. Mt 13:4–9).

529   When you feel the urge to boast of your abilities, are provoked to quarrel, or feel anger, be silent. No matter how wise you may be, you might end up saying more hurtful things than you intended.

530   So many of your writings, so many of your speeches, so many of your programs and important projects which have achieved success have been born from the secret recesses of your mind and heart. It is in the silent depths of your being that you discover the fundamentals: sacrifice, patience, reflection, and love.

531   Prudence is not secretive; it is simply common sense and judicious behavior. For example, you would not want people to expose your private life in public discussion. But when you are frequently reminding others to keep the secrets you have divulged, aren't you betraying all secrets by proving yourself incapable of keeping confidences?

CHAPTER 22

Joy

Offer the gift of happiness to one another.

532   Holiness does not consist in putting on long faces or being sad and miserable. Holiness is continuously joyful because it is the possession of God.

533   Do not be downhearted. Have a supernatural outlook and you will see everything in a new light.

534   Why are you unhappy? Perhaps something is disturbing your relationship with God. Examine yourself at once to discover what it is.

535   You should always be joyful. The Road of Hope does not allow for traveling in sadness; it is the road that restores joy.

536   How is it that you feel discouraged if you are working for God? The more difficult things are, the happier you should be, just as John and Peter were when they

were flogged at the hands of the Sanhedrin. "So the apostles left the Sanhedrin, rejoicing that they had been considered worthy to be dishonored for the sake of the Name" (Acts 5:41); or like Paul, "I am wonderfully encouraged and despite all our afflictions I am brimming over with joy" (2 Cor 7:4).

537 When you are successful give thanks to God, and when you are a failure give thanks to God. Rejoice always! When you fail, you will soon see if you serve God or your own will. To be joyful and courageous in a moment of failure is more difficult than in a moment of good fortune. You could count heroes of the former kind on the fingers of one hand.

538 If you are always morose, pessimistic, and complaining, people will begin to doubt the eloquent advice you constantly offer. Seeing your example, would they be able to put their faith in the God you witness to?

539 Be happy with those who love you, with those who hate you, when your heart suffers deeply, when everyone follows you, when you are alone and abandoned. Be joyful and help everyone you meet to experience this same joy, even when you may feel brokenhearted. To act in this way requires more virtue than all the acts of fasting and self-denial put together.

540 You have no money? You have no gift to give? You have nothing at all? You are forgetting that you have the gift of happiness to give to others, the gift of peace which this world cannot give, the treasure of joy which knows no bounds.

541   How can you rid yourself of sadness? Pray! And why pray? Because in prayer you meet the Lord, just as Mary Magdalene met him while she searched for his body, or as the two disciples met him on the road to Emmaus, where they soon forgot their grief and distress (cf. Jn 20:18; Lk 24:33–35).

542   "Instead, rejoice insofar as you are sharing in Christ's sufferings, so that when his glory is revealed you may rejoice and exult" (1 Pet 4:13).

CHAPTER 23

Wisdom

The holy cross is the book that teaches true wisdom.

543   "For the message of the cross is foolishness to those who are on their way to destruction, but for those who are being saved — for us — it is the power of God" (1 Cor 1:18).

544   When people praise you or insult you, do not be anxious, on the one hand, because you fear you may lose something, or glad, on the other hand, because you may gain something. Neither is true. Nothing people say can increase or decrease your worth. Only failing to do God's will can harm you, and only the practice of virtue can benefit you. Be no more concerned about praise or criticism than you would be afraid of a toy gun or eager to possess counterfeit money.

545   Who will "pull down the mighty from their thrones"? (cf. Lk 1:52) Who will "scatter the arrogant of heart"?

(cf. Lk 1:51) Who will restore order to a world of confused and erroneous thoughts? Who will bring peace to the people of our time and reassure them as they travel along the Road of Hope? The only answer is God and the wisdom he bestows on us through the hands of Mary who is the "Seat of Wisdom."

546   The world of the poor writhes in hunger and thirst and is dragged in all directions by so many social problems which defy solution. Squalor imprisons wisdom! But the world of materialism wallows in a sea of pleasure and creates "needs" in society. Materialism causes greater confusion in our minds, and when it is elevated as the teacher of the whole world, it spreads disquiet and discord in society. Pride causes the loss of wisdom!

547   The world is changed by actions, but also by ideas. It is ideas which direct actions.

548   When scholars and scientists — who often believe that they know and have discovered everything — kneel in prayer to God and humbly acknowledge that their discoveries are a gift from God, then they will see that everything is arranged according to a perfect order and plan from all eternity.

549   Scientists and geniuses have contributed very much toward the advancement of civilization. But they possess only a small portion of the light and of the truth. A world of such splendid order as ours must have an overriding supreme wisdom. This wisdom is the Word:

"Through him all things were made" (*Nicene Creed;* cf. Heb 11:3).

550   "The Word became flesh" (Jn 1:14), and God the Father proclaimed, "This is My Beloved Son, in whom I am well pleased; hear him!" (Mt 17:5). He is the Way; follow only his footsteps. He is the Truth; believe only in the word he teaches. He is the Life; live only by his spirit (cf. Jn 14:6).

551   Do not become doubtful because the people "the world" considers wise fail to find the Road of Hope. The Lord has forewarned us: "I praise you, Father, Lord of heaven and earth, because You hid these things from the wise and intelligent, and revealed them to babes" (Mt 11:25). Thank God for having bestowed his true wisdom on you.

552   "The world" fears this wisdom, which the Lord called "the narrow way," because it upsets our old way of life. It rebukes "the world," overturns former values, and is hard for human nature to accept. But in every period of history, humble souls of good will and those "little ones" fired with youthful enthusiasm have followed this wisdom to the end.

553   The wisdom which the Holy Spirit bestows will enlighten your projects, guide your plans, and transform your actions by giving them an eternal value. It will convert you into an immortal child of the Holy Spirit.

554 Have confidence and follow Paul's example: "When I came to you, I did not proclaim the mystery of God to you in high-sounding language or with a display of wisdom. I had made up my mind to know nothing while I was among you except Jesus Christ, and the fact that he was crucified" (1 Cor 2:1–2).

555 The crucifixion of the Lord is the wisdom that comes from heaven. The experience of the last twenty centuries shows that it accomplished a brilliant revolution that cannot be concealed, and whose power cannot be held back. Many courageous people have volunteered to live in the service of this wisdom.

556 If you desire wisdom, you must pray earnestly for it and entrust your whole life unreservedly to the will of God. When you encounter a crisis, even one that brings you before a court, it will not be you who speaks, but the Holy Spirit will speak through you. Remember that when Stephen preached he was "filled with the Holy Spirit" (cf. Acts 6:9 –10).

CHAPTER 24

Study

To study is to pray.

557   If you wish to advance and make rapid and solid progress on the Road of Hope, you must study.

558   The time of study is a time of prayer.

559   "You shall love the Lord your God with your whole heart and with your whole soul and with your whole strength and with your whole understanding" (Lk 10:27). Not to study in order to increase the level of your service to others indicates that you still do not really love God.

560   Study in order to understand. Study in order to reform. Study in order to serve. Study in order to love.

561   Whoever has been given ten gold coins must earn ten more; whoever has been given five coins must earn another five; whoever has been given one coin must

also earn one more (cf. Lk 19:13–25). You have a grave responsibility to study when you are in a position to do so.

562   Study does not necessarily mean joining a class or becoming a student of literature or science. Study means the exercise and improvement of your abilities, the perfection of your work and keeping pace with the modern world.

563   It is true that God's grace is needed to effect a world revolution, but you must also become a competent instrument.

564   When a person with great responsibility lacks competence, great disasters can occur. Would you put your life in the hands of an inexperienced pilot or doctor?

565   Look upon your work as a vocation to carry out the will of God within society and society will be sanctified.

566   To make sacrifices for your profession, to be diligent regarding cultural affairs, to serve the cause of science are all highly commendable efforts. But remember that these are the means, not the end.

567   Put your knowledge into practice. Theory and practice are not mutually exclusive. Practice leads you closer to reality, and you will discover that things are more easily said than done. Learning from this observa-

tion, you will be less critical of others and increase your self-examination.

568 The Church needs intelligent minds to carry the love of God to every part of the world. Yet the Church also suffers and is disturbed by the division and confusion caused by those whose intelligence is accompanied by arrogance and conceit. The fallen angels behaved in just this way.

569 Laziness is the root of all evil. The true apostle is incapable of laziness. There are no retired apostles, but only apostles who are able to adapt their methods of working according to their capabilities and strength.

570 When you are young, your life is filled with hope, you are fervent in the practice of virtue, and you work to improve your talents. You experience encouragement and all your efforts give you a sense of bright optimism regarding your apostolic ideals.

571 If you went up in an airplane and looked down on the scene below: the traffic, houses, people, and various objects, they would appear as children's toys. If you went to the moon you would see how tiny the earth is. The more you study and increase your knowledge, the more you realize how much there is yet to learn.

572 The Church is in the midst of a society where the whole of knowledge and science should be employed to

defend and present the truth. The greater your knowledge, the more capably will you serve the Church.

573   The more knowledgeable we become, the more we realize our limitations. Only ignorant people believe their knowledge is unlimited.

574   Many intellectual Catholics conceal the Catholic side of their characters in their social and academic life. These are the "shirt" Catholics; they put on or take off their Catholicism like a shirt, according to convenience.

575   Imagine what progress you would have made by now if you had memorized just one thought every day or read just one extra book every month. If you have not done these things up till now, begin at once today.

576   If you are not an expert, it is easy to be pretentious and to make foolhardy statements. If you find yourself in a high position, it is even easier to create the illusion of actually being an expert. Your inability in such circumstances would be all the more deplored because of the great disasters you could bring upon yourself and many others.

577   To be talented is insufficient; it is also necessary to be virtuous. The talented yet proud and hard-to-please person only uses his or her talents to deal with material things. Such a person lacks the sensitivity required in dealing with human relationships where he or she might have to please and persuade others.

578   To consider yourself a specialist in every field is an out-of-date attitude. Today if you wish to serve, you will need to enlist the cooperation of people from every branch of knowledge.

579   A diploma attests to the fact that you possessed a particular level of knowledge, especially at the time of final examinations. If your studies were to stop there, even a pile of diplomas would not guarantee your continued expertise in a particular field.

580   How long do you have to study? You must study continually. The world is changing; the work of the Church is ever new and fresh; the instruments of the Church are constantly in need of being sharpened. God does not bestow the wisdom of Solomon or the understanding of Mary on uncommitted people.

581   You will understand a truth when you seek to study that truth. When you devote yourself to defending that truth, you will understand it more thoroughly.

CHAPTER 25

Progress

*Humanity has the honor
of liberating the world.*

582   Progress is not only concerned with feeding and clothing humanity, or expanding agricultural methods, with the sinking of wells or the digging of canals. It also means the promotion of human dignity in every way so that all people may live in a manner more befitting their dignity.

583   Do not be content with simply helping someone, with exercising the easiest form of charity: almsgiving. God requires that you do something more difficult by helping others in such a way that they may be enabled to help themselves and in turn to one day help others.

584   God desires our collaboration in his work of creation and redemption. If God works alone, the work

will be perfect, but humanity will be less noble. Follow God's method!

585   We are called to withdraw and de-emphasize our own importance upon the completion of a task by Christ's profound and very meaningful teaching: "We are servants of no special merit; we only did what we should have done" (Lk 17:10). This stems from our being the instruments through which the grace of God operates. As God's instruments, it is futile for us to seek gratitude or to keep others dependent upon us — they have already been set free.

586   Allow others to advance, and yield your position to them. Demand more of them, but give them no less of yourself. Teach others to be of help. Do not take pride in your role as a benefactor, but be a true neighbor to everyone and serve everyone.

587   No matter how better off others may be because of your assistance, you have not brought about their true advancement if they have become mindless.

588   The tragedy of poverty lies not only in destitution, but in the fact that people cannot live in a way befitting their dignity.

589   Supervisor and employee, officer and private soldier, teacher and student, differ from one another in position, but these differences are only superficial. The essential point is that we travel in company with one another because we are human, and because we are all children of God. "I no longer call you servants, because the servant does not know what his lord does. I have called you friends because everything I have heard from the Father I have made known to you" (Jn 15:15).

590   The best gift you can give your employee is not an expensive item of clothing, a good pair of shoes, or a valuable watch. The most precious gift you can give is your humanity: fraternal love offered quietly in small gestures throughout the day.

591   God could have chosen passive people to cooperate with him in his work, but instead he has chosen sinners with their impetuosity and complexities of character.

592   It is easy to train people to choose the path of least resistance, to only wish to follow, to be helped, to be rescued in difficulties, to only receive what you have to offer. This will make you their indispensable leader, and you will find yourself needed by such people forever. Rather, you should train responsible people, those who wish to stand on their own two feet and whose behavior accords with their human dignity.

593   As difficult as it is, you should motivate yourself to help others to stand on their own, to think for themselves, to organize themselves, to fight for themselves, and if need be, to question your ideas. You will be really happy to find them progressing along with you rather than following you.

594 Nuclear power is an enormous discovery that our times can be proud of. But few people use this power for the purpose of peace and progress. Fewer still know how to worship and praise the power of God who gave us this resource. However, there are many people who use this gift of the heavenly Father to manufacture weapons of destruction that become more frightful every day.

595 Humanity offends God grievously when it abuses his gifts by employing them for unjust purposes and terrible acts of fratricide.

596 The world has run out of living space, the human heart has become too crowded. We do not have to fear that the world's food supply is insufficient, but that humanity is on the verge of devouring itself with a ferocity that exceeds that of wild beasts.

597 Lectures on the drought in Sahel, or the unrest in Bangladesh, or the violence in South America are well and good. But you must recognize the Lord Jesus Christ in the person of your neighbor who is abandoned, and that the Gospel is not preached enough in your surroundings, in the house next door, or under your very own roof. When the human heart has exhausted its love and the turbulence of selfish revenge has taken over, then disaster is not far off.

598 Humanity takes pride in the power of the atom, the new forms of energy, the increased effectiveness of weapons, spacecrafts capable of reaching the far ends of the universe…we live in an era of boundless possibilities. However, if humanity abandons the purpose which is at the root of development and forgets God who is the "maker of heaven and earth, of all that is seen and unseen" *(Nicene Creed),* then human pride could reduce the earth to dust and ashes.

599　The hunger, thirst, and utter misery of poor nations is a tragedy. But the greater tragedy is that there are nations of the world that are oblivious to the enslavement and exploitation of these poor nations.

600　"Progress is the new term for peace" (Pope Paul VI).

601　So long as developed nations fail to set aside at least one percent of their incomes to help poorer countries; so long as the rich who constitute 20 percent of the world's population are in complete possession of 80 percent of the world's resources, the danger of nuclear war cannot be avoided.

602　A plan for aiding underdeveloped nations which does not exploit its recipients would have more prospects for restoring peace than conferences on limiting nuclear weapons or economic summit meetings. These are simply a waste of time and money because no one trusts anyone else at such meetings.

603　Pope Paul VI urged us to be apostles of progress. Indeed, he was the "traveling pope" for progress and peace.

604   "Progress" could describe a world in which the last will and testament of Jesus is being realized. All people would love one another, help one another, and share with one another in a spirit of universal brother and sisterhood.

CHAPTER 26

Dedication

*Your standard of dedication
should be such that you are willing
to lay down your life as Jesus did.*

605   Dedication does not consist in throwing oneself into
feverish activity. Dedication is more profound. It means
following the example of the Lord, loving to the point
of being forgetful of self for the sake of others, offering
oneself without reservation so as to be united with others in order that they be enriched and that God's work in
them may bear fruit.

606   Humanity is like God only when people are continuously self-giving after the example of the Persons of
the Blessed Trinity in their total self-donation, complete
relationship, and absolute love.

607   In harmony with the will and grace of God, you
must become your true self: the image of God within
you that is perhaps obscured by dust and camouflage.

Like a sculptor chiseling and filing away at a piece of rock, gradually the Lord's features will take shape.

608   When you help others to forget themselves so that they may truly dedicate themselves, you are helping the image of God within them to be manifest.

609   The moment of self-offering is itself a lesson in sacrifice. To speak of self-offering is easy, but the reality is difficult. To convince a person to offer him or herself may take a long time, but the act of offering takes an instant. There are many people who call for self-sacrifice, but to persevere in self-sacrifice is very rare.

610   The many occasions that present themselves during the day for renewed dedication are not occasions of suffering or of loss. Rather, they are a challenge from God for you to grow.

611   You must be traveling on the Road of Hope in order to dedicate yourself and to invite others to dedicate themselves. The finest service you can render is to help others to grow in their resemblance of the image of God in Christ.

612   "This is how we came to know love — he laid down his life for us; we too should lay down our lives for others" (1 Jn 3:16). "What is the measure of self-giving?" you ask. Do as Jesus: lay down your life. If you have to make grand announcements about what you are doing, however, and your activities lack commitment; if you are careless in the practice of your faith and fear hunger, poverty, imprisonment, or death; if you dedicate yourself to saving those who have already won the battle, then it would be better to cease your involvement because your dedication is a sham. Your only concern is the commercial aspect: what dividend you will derive from your investment.

613 Do not do things for yourself alone, but for others also; do not desire to dedicate yourself only, but desire that others dedicate themselves as well; do not seek affection only for yourself, but, as a stone thrown into the water sends out continuous ripples in ever-widening circles, urge others to open wide the circle of their affection to include their neighbors. Do these things to draw out of people the nobility of the humanity God willed from all eternity.

614 Why do you feel that your life is incomplete, that it has lost its direction? Why do you feel so agitated and weak? Perhaps it is because you have not yet dispersed the heavy black cloud eclipsing the image of God in you.

615 Many others around you, in fact the whole of humanity, painstakingly fight their way through the mist. Dedicate your life to building a bridge of hope to connect them to God who is their supreme goal, everlasting love, and fulfillment. In God, no human being is estranged from another, but each one is everyone's brother or sister.

616 Some people close their eyes or turn their faces in order to avoid seeing, some people stop their ears in order to avoid hearing. However, truth is still truth. Look clearly, listen carefully, and learn reality from your neighbor, who is your teacher.

617 Sociologists and psychologists analyze human reality through laborious studies and statistical estimations according to their respective disciplines. Do not disregard these scientific projects. Rather, gather up the questions they raise and read them through the eyes of faith.

618 If you open your eyes, you will observe the hundreds of thousands of youth being neglected and living without a future. They continually discuss their dream of building a new society, a new humanity. But their dream is lost in their experiences with drugs, violence, vice, lies, and discouragement. They need you and their appeal to you is like the cry of a drowning person, the entreaty of one who is suffocating.

619 You should be aware of the various ways that people dedicate themselves to apostolic work. There are some people who freely and wholeheartedly dedicate themselves, yet after a time they are inclined to doubt the value of their struggle. They lose heart and retreat into the consolation of private prayer saying, "I am afraid of forgetting God." But they should persevere both in prayer and active commitment. Others throw their whole soul and body into the struggle and, to free their hands for the fight, dispense with God completely.

At first they think, "When I succeed, then I will remember God." But they end up saying, "This is entirely the work of human beings. I am the one who makes all the effort, it has nothing to do with God, so leave him out of it." There are still others who do not give up, or flee the battlefield, or betray the mission which God entrusted to them. They firmly believe that they will be victorious only with Christ, and so they say with all their hearts, "I dedicate myself to Christ."

620   Are you the kind of pious Catholic who spends so much time in the shadow of a church that you seem to have become part angel, part saint, and little remains of the human? Follow Jesus who is true God and true man. Become fully human again.

621   Do you leave everyone else to do the work of building up the world day by day, while you fail to discover what this means or remain unaware and uninvolved? The Lord has redeemed you, entrusted you with a mission, and placed you in the world in this particular century, this decade, this milieu. The Lord put *you,* a human being, not a rock, into all of this. There is a big difference!

622   The most disastrous scandal of our time is the separation of the practice of faith within the church from its practice in society.

623   Although you may not be able to fathom it, an effective revolution capable of renewing the world begins in your own heart and reaches all the political,

economic, and social structures. It cannot be realized without God or without humanity — in Christ and with Christ. Dedicate yourself to this revolution.

624 For a long time now I have watched you come close to God, but you do not see him, you do not meet him, you do not converse with him, you do not act with him. You dedicate yourself without thought of God but are not at peace in your soul because you confine him to a church.

625 As a Christian your dedication must be unique, because you view the end and means from faith. Your end is to love God in your neighbor for the sake of Christ. Your means are the existing organizations and structures you cooperate with sincerely, not manipulating them. You love and do not hate, you do not take advantage of others, you do not rebel.

626 Choose a way of dedicating yourself based on your ability, the needs of your neighbor, and the milieu in which you live. You cannot do everything, but do everything you can with faith.

627 Although being an apostle means that you follow a path of wholehearted dedication to apostolic activities of a religious nature, this should not prevent you from serving your neighbor in mundane affairs according to the needs and circumstances in which Divine Providence has placed you.

628   If you lead a life of faith, you will see events with the eyes of Jesus and you will perceive their eternal dimensions.

629   When you read or hear the daily news, step beyond the human and historical aspects and be convinced that "this is the news of the kingdom of heaven." Then, after folding up your newspaper or turning off your radio or television, pray in a heartfelt manner.

630   Behind the newsprint, television screen or radio waves, you will discover the Gospel values in events. You will experience joy and hope in positive events which are advantageous to the People of God, as well as anxiety and sorrow at those events which are a hindrance to the People of God on their journey to the Promised Land.

631   We use various terms to distinguish between the spiritual and the temporal, between the soul and the body. But these elements cannot be separated from each other; they are bound together in the heart of a child of God, so that life and history are as one. The spiritual and temporal, the soul and body are intimately linked together.

632   The secret of studying events in a perceptive way is to nourish your soul with the Gospel. Being united with Jesus gives you his spirit, and so you will study events and ask, "How does God look at the world?" "God the

Father so loved the world that he gave his only Son to redeem the world" (cf. Jn 3:16).

633   At every moment, you are carrying out God's plan in history.

CHAPTER 27

Renewal

Prepare for a new Pentecost in the Church.

634   Renewal is a return to the sources. Renewal is meant to help us as Catholics to return to the fullness of the Catholic faith and as Christians to return to Christ. Gandhi often made this thought-provoking remark: "I love Christ, but I do not love Christians because they are not Christ-like."

635   Renewal does not mean simply changing externals. It does not mean changing some of the ritual to render it more attractive, or the names of committees to render them more appealing, or destroying old structures and raising some new organizations or holding meetings, or issuing manifestoes. Paul states clearly what renewal means: "Put off your old self, your former way of life which is corrupted by deceitful desires! Be renewed in your mind and spirit and clothe yourself with the new self created in accordance with God's design in true righteousness" (Eph 4:22–24).

636　　People often accuse the Church of being slow to move, old-fashioned, and weighed down by structures — and so it is not surprising to find it in crisis. This is not true. Do not raise a cry against the Church in order to excuse yourself from self-examination and reflection. The Church is the entire People of God, which includes you. However, if there is a crisis, these are the causes:

1) a decrease in valuing and emphasizing prayer;
2) a lost sense of identity: Catholics are no longer distinguishable from others in society;
3) a lack of an acceptance of the folly of the Lord's cross.

637　　In the context of renewal, people have consumed much paper and ink writing about "returning to the sources." But consideration is superfluous without action. What did the first Christians do? They were strongly moved by Christ's will which always stayed fresh in their minds and which was summed up by one word, love. In this way the revolution of love reformed the whole Greco-Roman empire, transformed its very foundations, and stripped away the old humanity to replace it with a new model and a new society.

638　　Human love is limited to one group of people. Spiritual love embraces everyone. Human love returns love with love. Spiritual love makes the initiative to love. Human love is drawn especially toward oneself. Spiritual love unites with others. Human love is touching.

Spiritual love is completely transforming. When human beings change, society will change, law will change, communications between peoples will change. This is total renewal.

639 In order to renew ourselves, we must return to the ultimate source, that is, God. How do the Scriptures speak of God? John tells us that "God is love" (1 Jn 4:8). Jesus said, "The Father and I are one" (Jn 10:30). He desires that our renewal be according to his will: "I give you a new commandment — love one another; as I have loved you, you too should love one another" (Jn 13:34) and "So that all may be one, just as you, Father, are in me and I in You" (Jn 17:21). Love and unity!

640 How long must we be engaged in renewal? Constantly! We are always in need of beginning again. We always have to be aiming at our conversion. Do not be content if today you have not advanced one more step than yesterday in your union with God. You can be quite certain that the moment you stand still, you are beginning to slide back down the slope into your old habits.

641 You ask to what degree must you renew yourself. I want you to renew yourself to the degree of the perfection of Christ, according to the spirit of Paul — that is, you must reach a standard which cannot be improved, a standard in which your possessions cannot be reduced because you no longer have anything, a standard in which your sole wealth is Jesus Christ.

642   Be generous and single-hearted toward God so that you give yourself completely in whatever he desires. And do not forget the other aspect of accepting completely whatever God sends you.

643   Just as a sick child is restored to health by a blood transfusion from his parents, so you and the Church receive new life from the continuous outpouring of Christ's blood into your veins and heart.

644   Every day the press emphasizes sensational events and political upheavals. You should be aware of these events in order to share in humanity's anxieties. These should also have a positive effect. They should urge you to build a new world in which the press will not find such events to report on. You have to build the kingdom of God right now in this world with all the means at your disposal.

645   Every period of history experienced the Good News through the people Divine Providence gave to the world at that time, people such as Benedict, Augustine, Francis of Assisi, Bernard, Vincent, Teresa of Avila, Ignatius, John Bosco, Thérèse of Lisieux, and so many others. Each one, in his or her time, stressed an aspect of the Gospel and a new way of living it which corresponded to the needs of that particular moment.

646   Every day, re-evangelize your mind and heart by means of spiritual reading and meditation. Immerse yourself in the everlasting Word so that the Gospel will gradually permeate and take deep root in every cell and fiber of your being. That is true renewal, and the most enduring revolution.

647   What will become of all our endeavors for renewal, with all the organizations and committees and their actions as well as their sacrifices? What is to become of humanity with all the machinery, factories, highways, spaceships, satellites, and other scientific achievements? What direction is our life going to take?

648   If we do not look to God as our source of ever new and consoling hope, who else can make sense of our life?

649   Begin today with your expression, your gestures, your silence, your heart, your soul, all your actions, your manner of living and of dying, to shed the light of God's presence within you on the places you go and the people you meet.

650   If you simply "keep the faith" you have not practiced renewal. While the devil desires to drive God out of the world and to drag it away from God, you must bring God to the world and lead it back to God.

651   People sacrifice everything for the sake of an ideal. The Christian and every Christian community that desires to serve all must live for one ideal: God.

652   The most impenetrable barrier is not a fortress or an electric fence, it is indifference. Others may be dying or suffering from hunger and misery, but you are unaf-

fected; in the face of the decadence and collapse of society, you are unconcerned. With such an attitude, how will you ever overcome barriers of indifference?

653 The renewal of society is accomplished by people who faithfully renew themselves according to the Gospel. Faith brings new value to their work, and while people may not know them well, or may never have heard them speak, they perceive something different in their more beautiful lifestyle.

654 Walking fast or rushing will not get you far, but only by walking firmly and purposefully will you advance. There is no need to make an urgent appeal to the world to advance. Begin to advance yourself.

655 Pope Paul VI clearly pointed out that if today's world is to be renewed, it must eliminate:

1) secularism, with its ultimate aim of temporary happiness, support of hedonism, the accumulation of possessions, power, and influence;
2) "worldliness" which no longer recognizes the values of sacrifice, humility, or patience;
3) the belief that politics alone can solve all the problems concerning peace, progress, families, brotherhood, and justice.

656 Is your life merely a continuous chain of events with time for sleeping, for rising, for eating, for study, for work, for relaxation, watching television, or reading newspapers? If there is no unifying element to your life, it will be meaningless. That element is the love of God. With it your life will change and all your actions will testify to God's presence within you.

657   Cooperate with others to bring about a new springtime in the Church. Prepare people to welcome a new Pentecost in the Church. Become the door that opens to receive the cool gust of wind blowing in to regenerate the Church.

658   If you do not advance along the Road of Hope or aim at holiness, you belong to neither the younger nor the older generation, but to the generation of the dead. How wonderful and attractive it would be if, in this age of weakness, there should arise a generation of saints! God desires this, and you should desire it for your own life.

659   Renewal demands courage and determination. In the presence of so much suffering, do not be indifferent and pretend that you do not see this suffering. In the face of God's call, do not pretend that you have not heard. Be a dedicated apostle of the work of renewal and, with patient self-sacrifice, a lover of the Church.

660   The driving force and author of all renewal in the Church is the Holy Spirit "who renews the face of the earth" (cf. Ps 104:30). Renewal is a new Pentecost and there can be no new Pentecost without the Holy Spirit. Without the Holy Spirit, there can be no renewal.

661　　Update yourself. Strive unceasingly to improve your announcement of the Good News so that it reaches into every heart and every family.

662　　Renewal involves making the Gospel relevant for today's world. The Church does not dilute the message of the Gospel, but she presents the Gospel to today's people in contemporary language. If the Church does not go to the people, the people will not come to the Church.

663　　Do you pay attention to the concerns of "the world" or do you lock yourself up in your own little ghetto? Are you patiently helping to build a new society — brick by small brick — or are you still following the old road of negative criticism?

CHAPTER 28

New Life

Christians, do not be sad like those
who have no hope (cf. 1 Thes 4:13).

664 People who have lost their way or have no goal tend to lose hope. People who advance toward their goal have hope. For the Christian the goal is to meet God, the loving Father who awaits all his children. In his presence, all hope is fulfilled.

665 The person without an eternal goal approaches the hour of death as a time of hopelessness, because it means the loss of pleasure and of friends. Death means the collapse of his or her world, a void of darkness. But for the believer, the end of the Road of Hope is bathed in light.

666 Think a moment of all the drops of rain that fall heavily on a winter's afternoon. Every day as many people enter eternity with scarcely anyone taking notice. Someday you will be as one of those drops of rain.

667   While other people may have regrets or complain as they face the end of their life, you should be eager to proclaim "the joyful hope of the coming of our Lord Jesus Christ."

668   While people who are concerned only with this world may say, "Every day brings me one step closer to the grave," you should say, "Every day brings me one step closer to the gate of heaven."

669   What "worldly people" regard as death, you should consider life. What they call their last breath, you should call the first breath of your new life. What they call the end, you should call the beginning.

670   Be prepared and hold the lamp of faith in your hand as you await the day of the Lord's return — however, wherever, and whenever he wishes.

671   When a child is temporarily in another's care and hears his parents returning, he drops everything without hesitation and runs to them. Likewise, we, in our temporary earthly abode, should detach ourselves from everything without regret and run to the arms of our eternal Father.

672   Knowing that this world is only our temporary home, why give such importance to a particular place, work, or position? Why regret the loss of any object — this table or that chair? Do you imagine that you will be able to take them along with you to enjoy eternal happiness? How absurd to consider such a thing!

673   Many prayers conclude with the words: "lives and reigns forever and ever." What hope these words should bring to Christians, but because we have become so accustomed to them, we give little attention to their eternal significance.

674   In the face of life's innumerable trials and tribulations, fervently believe in and frequently recite: "I believe in the resurrection of the body and life everlasting" *(Apostles' Creed)*. Therein lies the secret of Christian courage.

675   From the many people who spent so much time and money on their beauty and health and yet who have died nonetheless, we can have some idea of the "nothingness" of the material world.

676   Do not be so unwise as to leave to the last moment of your life any regret for times you have exchanged true riches for tawdry imitations.

677   When apostles reach heaven, they continue assisting the world. Their work is no longer hampered by the constraints of the physical fatigue suffered in this life.

678   Apostles do not die; their life "is changed, not ended" *(Preface for the Dead)*. "Right now we see indistinctly, as in a mirror, but then we will see face to face" (1 Cor 13:12).

679 In the midst of hardships, oppression, deception, and injustice, stand firm and proclaim with the whole People of God: "He shall come again in glory to judge the living and the dead and his kingdom will have no end" *(Nicene Creed)*.

680 You feel consoled because you will be judged by your merciful Father. The more just he is, the more reassured you are, for he will take your frailty into account. However, do not abuse God's goodness by foolishly allowing yourself to remain in sin.

681 God calls you to be a saint. If you choose not to answer the call, you show no gratitude for God's love and mercy.

682 In the midst of the most terrible trials, remember the Book of Revelation: "He will wipe every tear from their eyes and death shall be no more — no more grief or crying or pain, for what came before has passed away" (Rev 21:4).

683 Lucia, Jacinta, and Francisco were filled with terror and fear after they had seen hell in a vision at Fatima. They could never forget that spectacle. Believe the words of our Lady; do not blind yourself to the existence of hell.

684 The most up-to-date and useful tool for making important decisions is called "eternity." Is it to be an eternity of love in heaven or an eternity of hatred without God?

685   The attitude of the early Christians toward death was completely new in its day. Their witness converted the Roman world to belief in the love of God and eternal life.

686   The transience of this life should not be a motive for escaping "the world" or neglecting your responsibilities. Rather, it should be an encouragement for you to engage in an enthusiastic competition with time. For some, "Time is money," but you must be convinced that time is heaven, time is love.

687   Anything that does not bear the trademark "eternity" is counterfeit.

688   The grain of rice sown in the field is not dead; from it, there will arise abundant new life. The grain of rice cooked as food also does not die; it lives on in a different, more beautiful, more noble way.

689   On the wreaths with which you honor the dead, do not write the words, "Sincere Sympathy." In your letters do not continually use the word "deceased," for they "are resting in the hope of rising again" and enjoying the beatific vision of God.

690   For Christians there are no dead. All those who have died are living — they are living members of the Body of Christ just as we are. We are united with one another in faith.

CHAPTER 29

Suffering

If you wish to avoid suffering,
do not expect to become a saint.

691   The typhoon that sweeps through the trees breaks off the dry and rotted branches, but it cannot uproot the cross that is planted deep in the earth. Do not regret the loss of dead branches. Even if there had been no wind, they would still have fallen or been cut off since their presence is harmful to the entire tree.

692   Wherever Jesus went there were those who were willing to live and die for him and those who were determined to kill him. Why then do you expect everyone to love you, or become discouraged when someone hates you?

693   On the road along which you travel there are fragrant flowers and beautiful scenery, but there are also thorns and brambles; there are kind friends, but also enemies; there are times of rainfall, but also times of

burning heat. Be ready for both the pleasant and the unpleasant. Continue on the road and be filled with the Lord like Francis or Clare. Do not stop or be afraid of criticism, or waste time chasing after praise.

694   When you are overwhelmed by your suffering, look to the crucifix, embrace the crucifix, and then stand silently and steadfastly like Mary.

695   In the midst of your trials consider this suffering compared with heaven. This is God's way: blessed are the poor, those who weep, those who suffer persecution, the kingdom of heaven is theirs (cf. Mt 5:3–10).

696   You complain that others are not grateful to you. Did you do them a favor only to be thanked by them?

697   You complain that others constantly oppose you and dispute with you, and so impede your apostolic work. Have you forgotten the parable of the wheat and the weeds? (cf. Mt 13:24–30) The wheat of your good works will continue despite obstacles.

698   Are your activities curtailed, your reputation on the decline, opposition building up on all sides? Wait for God's time. "And every branch that does bear fruit he will prune so it will bear more fruit" (Jn 15:2). The green branch comes into bud and blossom, and brings forth an abundant harvest.

699   During his agony in the garden, our Lord took along the three apostles for whom he had a special affection:

Peter, James, and John (cf. Mt 26:37–38). Are you afraid to be one of his closest friends?

700　In times of suffering there are things to remember and things to avoid. Do not ask who was at fault but give thanks to God for the instrument that may sanctify you. Do not seek human consolation, but turn above all to our Lord in the Blessed Sacrament and to our Lady with your problems. When something has passed, do not mention it again, but cease all recriminations and rancor; forget about it, and say: "Alleluia!"

701　Are you angry because it is impossible to reason with your enemies? Do not be surprised, for "they persecuted the prophets before you in the same way" (Mt 5:12).

702　If you want to avoid suffering, do not expect to become a saint.

703　God uses trials and sufferings to teach us to better understand and be more compassionate with the suffering of others, just as Jesus prayed for humanity with "loud cries and tears" (cf. Heb 5:7).

704　In heaven you may say with regret, "How I wish I had had more opportunities to love God and suffer for him!"

705　You suffer most when you suffer at the hands of those who should understand and sympathize with you, indeed those who have the obligation to defend you.

Unite yourself with Jesus who hung on the cross and cried: "My God, my God, why have You forsaken me?" (Mt 27:46).

706   If you unite yourself with the passion of Jesus in your suffering, not only will you experience help in being courageous and patient, but your suffering will also have considerable redemptive value.

707   If you feel tense, rest for a while. If you can forget your worries, you will regain your strength and your work will be more effective. To accept that there is a limit to your strength is a sign of courage; to know how to look after your health is a sign of wisdom.

708   Time is an important factor, but do not be too hasty. Consider things patiently and wait. Often, time will help you to see things more objectively and with more clarity.

709   "Even if someone paid thousands of dollars a day to nurse these sick, I would not accept the offer," a doctor was once overheard saying. A religious sister replied: "As for me, Doctor, if not for the love of God, I would not do this work either — even if I were paid a million dollars an hour. But for God, I will stay here until death."

710   Suffering is the lot of humanity. However, Christian lives proclaim the Lord's death and acknowledge his resurrection. These words fill us with joy.

711   Do good, but do not publish it.

712   Perhaps you are furious at an incident which breaks your heart, and you protest its injustice. Now, consider what sins Jesus committed to deserve crucifixion. Do you think he was treated fairly?

713   A rose or lily are beautiful and sweet-scented so long as they receive compost, which decays to feed them and to help them produce blossoms. Apostolic work is also nourished when suffering feeds love.

714   The trial of suffering is the "permit" to follow the Lord and to enjoy happiness with him. "If any want to be my followers, let them deny themselves, take up their cross and follow me" (Mt 16:24).

715   There is no suffering so great as that of Jesus on the cross. As he was at the point of breathing his last, Jesus experienced in the depth of his soul a sense of abandonment by the Father. Jesus was crushed by the burden of the greatest ignominy in his life. He was compelled to cry out, "My God, my God, why have You forsaken me?" (Mt 27:46). During the most terrible and darkest moments of your life, unite yourself with Jesus. Peace will return and you will be able to say like Jesus, "Father, into Your hands I entrust my spirit!" (Lk 23:46).

716   Jesus asks you, "Can you drink the cup I am drinking, or be baptized with the baptism with which I am being baptized?" (Mk 10:38); to which you reply, "I volunteer to drink this bitter cup to the last drop because it is your cup and because you have drunk it before me!" The more bitter and fuller the cup, the greater will be the witness of your love. The more our Lord loves and trusts you, the more he desires to share this bitter cup with you.

717   Suffering is a heavy burden if, in fear, you attempt to avoid it. Suffering is a sweet experience if you courageously accept it.

CHAPTER 30

Childlike Happiness

The condition for entry into heaven:
"Become like children" (Mt 18:3).

718   An orphan who has everything could still be happy, but he will not know the same happiness enjoyed by a child with parents. However poor, a child who experiences love will be a happy child. Then realize that you are the happiest of children because you are a child of God the Father and a child of Mary.

719   When people apply for a job, they state their abilities and achievements. A little child simply declares, "I am the child of Mr. and Mrs. So and So of such and such a place." Be proud to say: "I am a child of God and a child of Mary."

720   If a little child goes to a shop to buy something for his mother, and finds that the shop has already closed, he knocks and knocks until finally the shopkeeper an-

grily opens the door prepared to scold the person knocking. When he sees the little child standing there, so simple and innocent, he changes his attitude and, full of smiles, embraces the child. "You poor little thing," he finally says, "you are such a good little child, what are you doing at this hour?" The little child obtains all he wants. Be like the little child with your Father.

721   A little child does not need to know whether her parents are rich or poor. She knows that she has a mother and father, and that is sufficient. If a bomb drops, a child experiences misery or danger, but if her parents are there, the little child will be able to fall asleep. A little child dwells, as it were, in the belief of her parents' all-powerful love. Your trust in God's all-powerful love should resemble that of a child in her parents.

722   No matter how many times a little child makes a mistake, the parents still love her because they know the child bears no malice. Although she keeps trying her best, things still go wrong, but it does not matter. Only her good will matters. She loves her parents, even if, as a child, she is weak. Likewise, God only asks for your good will; his grace will help you.

723   When you pray, do not be worried about how you will ask God for what you want. Keep your prayer simple and sincere, like that of a little child. A child knows that he is loved, so he confidently thrusts a hand into his father's pocket, or opens his mother's handbag looking for a present. Remember the Lord's

words about a child asking for bread and fish? (cf. Mt 7:9–10).

724   You are worn out, cannot concentrate, feel discouraged. It is of no consequence; so long as you love God, it is sufficient. When a child tires while playing in the presence of his parents, he falls sound asleep in his mother's arms.

725   When a little child has done something, or broken an object, he runs crying to his parents to confess his wrongdoing. Instead of regretting the loss of what has been broken, the parents embrace the child to comfort and soothe him. They value the child more than the object they lost. In the same way, you should be humble and sincere with God, and trust in his goodness.

726   God rejoices in our little sacrifices like a father who asks a child to share her candy. At first the child withdraws her hand and refuses to share, but on the father's insistence the little child, feeling very sorry, puts out her hand, gradually opens it, and gives some of her candy. Overjoyed, the father kisses the child for her generosity and for conquering her selfishness — and then gives the child even more.

727   The spiritual life of the child of God is not weak or passive. It follows a spiritual road which is easy amid difficulties, simple amid complexities, gentle yet determined, powerful in weakness, wise in foolishness. "Unless you turn about and become like children, you won't ever enter the kingdom of heaven!" (Mt 18:3).

728 The heart of a little child knows no hatred or indignation. When he is scolded by his mother, he cries, but he soon forgets his grief and will doze off in the arms of the one who just chastised him. Put aside all anger and animosity. Dwell in the gentle arms of your heavenly Father and you will always be happy.

729 Have no fear, it is the grace of God that makes saints. Be as fearless as a little child in her mother's arms, joyfully accepting the will of God, ready to follow it wherever it leads you, and loving God with all your heart. A little child would be willing to go up to the moon in a spaceship provided her parents traveled along.

730 Having the heart of a child does not mean being childish or naïve. It means to love without limit, to trust in God for everything, to do everything he commands, to give up everything to follow him, and to have absolute confidence in him. Be valiant and steadfast and you will be a worthy child of God and of Mary.

731 A little child does not keep anything for herself, but hands everything she is given over to her parents. Trust in God and Mary and you will have security and happiness.

732 God sees your heart and loves you as a Father. He rejoices in the small things you accomplish in his service as much as in the great, just as a mother rejoices as much in her child's first step as in his ability to win a race.

733   The secret of your strength on the Road of Hope is our Lord in the Eucharist and Mary our Mother.

734   Time and all creation belong to God; he is the Alpha and the Omega. God, the almighty and the supreme Lord of all, takes care of the birds of the air, the fish of the sea, the beasts of the jungle, and the flowers of the field; he counts the very hairs of your head. God is concerned only with love. Peace and happiness to the humble soul that longs for eternal love!

735   Our understanding of the way to heaven is so complex and difficult. Yet Jesus lays down only one condition: "Unless you turn about and become like children, you will not ever enter the kingdom of heaven!" (Mt 18:3).

736   Entrust everything to the hands of God, and then do not be afraid! There is nothing hard about that! Though you do not know where God is leading you — and you can be sure that he has unexpected things in store for you — it is enough to believe that God is your Father (cf. Mt 6:31–32).

CHAPTER 31

Charity

Charity is the hallmark of the Christian.

737   Before judging what course to take in any matter, pray. Then do as Jesus would do in your circumstances.

738   You are not necessarily practicing true charity just because you undertake some apostolic work in a far-off place. Only when you undertake such works in your own neighborhood, among the people you come in contact with daily, will I believe that you practice true charity.

739   Complaining is a highly contagious epidemic whose chief symptoms are pessimism, loss of interior peace, doubt, and a decrease in the zeal which comes from being united with God.

740   Making a donation, or buying a raffle ticket, or giving away some old clothes are the kinds of charitable acts we perform in order to avoid being hassled further.

Real love is difficult. Include your heart in your donations, in the raffle ticket, and in the parcel of old clothes.

741   You may say, "I cannot perform works of charity because I have no money." Why do you need money to practice charity? What about the charity of a smile, the charity of a handshake, the charity of compassion, the charity of a visit, or the charity of prayer?

742   Do not wait until you are about to die before you make peace with one another. Do not wait until you are near death to give away your possessions. An act of charity which is done simply because it cannot be avoided or done reluctantly only brings regrets, because it lacks the essential element of love.

743   People do not need your possessions or material help as much as they need your understanding and love.

744   You should not be angry when others criticize you; rather, you ought to be thankful that they do not mention any other faults and failings you have!

745   To live in a fraternal spirit is very beautiful. Our Lord said, "For where two or three are gathered in my name, I am there among them" (Mt 18:20). He knows how difficult this is, so he only demands the bare minimum of "two or three."

746   Living fraternally both tests and supports the spirit of charity. Trees in a forest support one another against being blown over when a storm strikes.

747   You cannot know the extent of damage someone may cause when in a drunken state, whether it be in the form of an accident, physical violence, or arson. In the same way, when you are filled with the desire for revenge, your powers of perception become even more impaired.

748   Our Lord enjoined his apostles to dress simply, but in clothing which is very difficult to find: "All will know by this that you are my disciples, if you have love for one another" (Jn 13:35).

749   Wherever love exists, God is there; wherever hatred exists, hell is there.

750   If you contrived to counsel your neighbors for the purpose of gaining information from them that you intended to reveal to others, your charity would be that of a secret agent.

751   In the space of a few seconds anyone could deface one of Raphael's masterpieces, which required great effort and so much time to create. And who could ever recreate Raphael's work? Just so a person's reputation may be destroyed forever.

752   Our Lord said, "So if you are presenting your offering at the altar and remember there that your brother or sister has something against you, leave your offering there before the altar and first go, be reconciled with your brother or sister, and then you can come and make your offering" (Mt 5:23–24). But you

do the opposite! You continue to offer your gift while airing the story of your disagreement to everyone except the person concerned. Such is your version of the Good News.

753   You maintain that there must be dialogue, yet refuse to allow anyone to express ideas contrary to your own. Such a dialogue is limited by a fixed agenda, or more correctly, it is two monologues.

754   You would regard as absurd a day-laborer who criticized the instructions of the engineer in a building project or a construction worker who criticized an architect's plans for the building of a house, or a medical assistant who criticized a surgeon's directions. Why then do you criticize your superiors who have more factors to consider than you imagine?

755   Love one another, not only by word, but also in deed (cf. 1 Jn 3:18). Love one another in such a way that "your left hand does not know what your right is doing" (cf. Mt 6:3). "Love one another as I have loved you" (Jn 15:12).

756   There are many types of charity. There is the noisy type of charity, broadcasting good deeds; the banker's charity that demands credit for everything done for another; the charity of a zookeeper that only involves food programs; the patronizing charity that looks down on those who receive; the dictator's charity that will only follow its own opinion; the charity of the fraud that must exhibit what it accomplishes.

757   The unjust word of a just man does endless damage. It is like poison dispensed at the hands of the doctor; the more it is spread, the more people it will kill.

758   People leading a religious life have only one possession they can call their own: their reputation. Anyone who violates that reputation is guilty of assassination.

759   If you praise those who praise you, accept those who accept you, and keep company with those who share your opinions, then you have neither charity nor wisdom. It is simply a case of the blind leading the blind.

760   A community that has an extremely "saintly" person will often find that person the unwitting cause of many martyrdoms.

761   If you would only put yourself in the place of others you would soon realize how careless and irresponsible your public statements may be, and you would become more prudent.

762   Things are easier said than done. People are very quick to condemn the present, to yearn for the past, and to applaud their own plans for the future. But when that future becomes the present, they forbid all criticism.

763   What kind of sense does it make to call your bad temper a virtue, and your neighbor's good will a fault or failing?

764 While you are aware of no shortage of defects in yourself, why are you so intent on attacking your neighbor's?

765 Love of neighbor is the most reliable test of your love of God.

766 To love others does not mean that you have to lavish signs of affection on them or spoil them; in fact, sometimes you may even have to cause them distress for the sake of truth or for their own good.

767 Jesus does not teach us to love by means of our emotions, since he tells us to love even our enemies. To love others means sincerely wishing them well and doing everything we can to secure their happiness. This demands that we forget ourselves completely.

768 You must be a gift in the hand of God that is ready to be presented by him to everyone without distinction. This is a gift everyone would love and desire.

769 The greatest mistake is failing to be aware that other people are Christ. There are many people who will not discover this until their last day.

770 If you examine the personality of every person you will find that no two people are alike. Do not generalize. The human personality is not a cassette tape that can be mass produced.

771   We must learn to thank one another — the recipient for the love and help received and the donor for the opportunity to grow in love.

772   Why do you set up court every day and force your neighbors to file through one by one? Why do I always see you sitting on the judge's bench, but never in the defendant's seat?

773   Replace your diplomatic smile with the smile of a sincere Christian.

774   Charitable and social works are both necessary and good. However, in this nuclear age, we cannot claim to have authentic love if we fail to dedicate ourselves to demanding the creation of new social structures, and/or changes in those which already exist, to secure a true liberation of humanity which would allow everyone to live more humanely.

775   It would be so wonderful if God had simply commanded us to love *him*. But he added our neighbor to the law of love and made this just as important as loving him. Many find this very difficult.

776   Why do you engrave the shortcomings of others on stone, and write your own sins only in sand?

777   The circumstances in which you find yourself may force you to be inactive. Nevertheless, continue to act in

a manner appropriate to the circumstances and spread love wherever you go. One day, when you look over the places you have been, you will be surprised to discover that the seeds of love you sowed have grown ten or one hundredfold in those whom Divine Providence allowed you to meet on the Road of Hope.

778   What is a fitting blessing for a community? "Blessed are those who are persecuted for doing God's will" (Mt 5:10). Yes, it is true — especially in those places where persecutions are systematically planned and carried out. Such persecutions bring redemption because they place you in an historic role within the Church's mission to change the world.

779   A true community is a united body. It does not treat its members as mere units, but as individual human beings.

780   Religious life once consisted of fasting, rising early in the morning, rising during the night, leading a life of silence. Today, religious life consists of living in a community, coming together for meetings, exchanging views, and working together.

781   Every night, before going to bed, you ought to be able to say, "I have loved all day today."

782   Anyone who makes false accusations against another person, reviles or stirs up hatred and opposition against that person — for whatever reason — cannot conceal his or her contradiction of the Gospel, because "God is love" (1 Jn 4:8).

783　Take a sheet of paper and calmly write down the virtues of those who annoy you and you will find that they are not as bad as you thought.

784　Why do you complain when people are ungrateful? Do you think your work goes unrewarded? Do you expect God to thank you? Remember, "insofar as you did it for one of these least of my brothers, you did it for me" (Mt 25:40).

785　Why are you so sparing in your praise of others, so slow to smile, or to simply shake a person's hand? There are so many people who are not looking for money; they only need your heart.

786　Unless your charitable works are done for God, you are no different than a paid social worker.

787　Charity knows no boundaries; if it has boundaries, it is no longer charity.

788　When you assist anyone, practice charity with your whole heart so that the recipient may forgive you for the uneasiness experienced on these occasions.

789　After the Lord performed a miracle for someone, he usually ordered that person to tell no one. There are many people who have never performed a miracle, yet tell everyone how charitable they are.

790   Do not complain that your coffee is bitter; it is your sugar that is not sweet enough!

791   A machine, no matter how solidly constructed, will break down if its parts are not oiled. Pour the oil of your charity into life so that it will run smoothly and not break down.

792   Charity is an extension of God's love for humanity.

793   As a Christian you should be able to say sincerely, "I do not regard anyone as my enemy, not even those who hate me most, those who persecute me, or those who desire my destruction. I always look on them as my own brothers and sisters."

794   If you are good, but others say you are bad, you are still good. If you are poor, but others praise you for being rich, you are still poor. So why are you concerned about the opinions of others?

795   People flatter themselves with regard to their imagined talents, spread rumors about their imagined achievements, or fabricate stories about the evildoing of their opponents. Do people really think they can fool God as well?

796   Men and women religious lead holy lives with the help of their particular religious exercises — communal fasting, self-denial, their Rule, recollection, etc. Lay people have one specific means: the practice of the virtue of charity.

797   Charity is the constant cultivation of the virtues connected with the heart, the mind, the temperament, the eyes, the ears, the tongue, etc. Even when your whole being rebels against it, your response should always be to love as Jesus would.

798   "In my Father's house are many rooms" (Jn 14:2). How penetrating is the Word of God! Treat everyone according to his or her personality and have respect for each individual person. Do not look on everyone as being exactly the same; human beings are not numbers or quantities. With human beings two plus two does not always equal four, just as with melons: two melons may equal four pounds, but sometimes it takes six melons to equal four pounds!

799   The practice of charity means that we become a community which produces new relationships. When there are new relationships, there will be a new world.

800   Charity not only means love and forgiveness, but also the creation of a new atmosphere in the local community, in the national community, and in the international community.

801   Charity changes the world of the children of men and women into the world of the children of God.

802   It is not enough to simply not hate. It is not enough merely to love others, or merely to help others. Only when love and action work in harmony is our love enough. Jesus prayed: "So that all may be one, just as

You, Father, are in me and I in You, so they, too, may be in us" (Jn 17:21).

803   Jesus was abandoned on the cross and he is still abandoned in every suffering brother and sister in the world.

804   The Lord will judge you on your practice of the virtue of charity, not on the huge successes you may have achieved.

805   Do not engage in the despicable practice of speaking evil of people who are not present. Speak as if your words were being recorded; act as if your actions were being photographed.

806   If you fail entirely to carry out the Lord's last testament — to live a life of charity — you will truly be a most ungrateful and unfortunate child of God.

CHAPTER 32

Ordinary Work

*Perform your ordinary work
in an extraordinary way.*

807   Your work may be small and your heart small, your work may be big and your heart big, your work may be big and your heart small, or the work may be small and your heart big. Let yourself be wholehearted in the smallest thing you do. To be faithful in big things is easy, but to be faithful in small things is difficult. Our Lord praised those who were faithful in little things (cf. Lk 16:10).

808   Viewed through the eyes of "the world," Mary's work was very ordinary: her assistance to Elizabeth, her care and concern for the infant Jesus in the manger, her duties at Nazareth, her journey to Jerusalem to worship in the temple, the burial of Joseph, the suffering and humiliation which she endured on Calvary…. But from a supernatural perspective her life was extraordinary, because everything she did was done for the love of Jesus.

809   To carry a baby is a common event, but when a baby is carried by his mother, it is an event filled with the utmost happiness for the baby.

810   "The guiding principle of my life is to accept everything with a humble heart, to think of a few ordinary ideas which could produce profound consequences" (Pope John XXIII).

811   There is no such thing as an unworthy work, only an unworthy heart.

812   With a noble heart an ordinary action can be ennobled. "Whoever gives a cup of water in my name will be rewarded in heaven" (cf. Mt 10:42).

813   In order for a person to be canonized it is necessary to prove that the candidate exercised heroic virtue. To persevere in our ordinary tasks throughout our life for the love of God is certainly heroic. This was the way of Thérèse of the Child Jesus.

814   If you wish to become a saint, do ordinary things well. They may seem so insignificant, but pour all your love into them.

815   If you look for the big things and despise the small ones, you will lose your way on the Road of Hope. The Lord has promised: "You were faithful over a few

things, so now I will set you over many. Come into your master's joy!" (Mt 25:21).

816   Whenever you look at a hundred-year-old tree, never forget that one hundred years earlier it was a tiny seed.

817   Can anyone reach the top of the Himalayan Mountains without first climbing their slopes? Likewise no one can reach the moon without special effort. Before attaining their goal, these people must train diligently every day and undergo trials and dangers.

818   You say you are waiting for the "right moment" to do something truly great. I wonder how many times such occasions will arise in your lifetime. No, take hold of the daily opportunities that arise to perform ordinary works in an extraordinary way.

819   Everyone who goes to the top of a Manhattan skyscraper praises its construction, but few stop to consider that the foundation which supports this edifice is built upon individual steel beams, pieces of gravel, and grains of sand.

820   The beauty of insignificant objects is magnified under a microscope. Do not despise small things.

821   A particular task may seem small, but by virtue of the sweat and tears involved in its execution, it is made precious. The work may be quite ordinary, but through dedicated love it becomes important. A devoted son

may continue to wear a very old woolen jacket, refusing to exchange it for a newer, more expensive one, because every stitch of wool in that garment is a sign of his mother's love for him.

822   Daily life is a succession of prayers of faith and love expressed in ordinary daily tasks.

823   A melodious piece of music can be broken down into simple notes, a marvelous painting into individual strokes, a beautiful tapestry into separate threads. But only a patient genius can create a masterpiece such as these.

824   Jesus used a child's five loaves of bread and two fish to perform a miracle to feed five thousand people (cf. Mt 14:17). The Lord is still almighty, but he depends upon your cooperation.

825   Those involved in events during the Lord's earthly life — the Samaritan woman he asked for water, the owner who lent his ass for Jesus to ride into Jerusalem, the man whose boat the Lord used to preach from, the owner of the room in which he instituted the Blessed Eucharist, the widow he watched drop her mite into the temple treasury — never guessed that they would one day receive honorable mention from our Lord (cf. Mt 21:2, 26:18; Mk 12:43; Lk 5:3; Jn 4:9).

826   A very ordinary action can produce a comforting atmosphere of love, without costing either money or great effort — and it usually goes unobserved. On the other hand, the moon may be beautiful, but no one lives there, because its atmosphere is inhospitable.

827   On the road which baptized people follow there is no ordinary action. Even the most trifling favor performed for another is a step toward love. And this love causes the human person to grow.

828   We know nothing about what the Lord, Joseph, and Mary did during the thirty years of the hidden life at Nazareth. In heaven we will have some understanding of their life.

829   We may assume, however, that those thirty years were filled with love, harmony, and unity beyond human understanding, because this is the mystery of God's love.

830   Thirty years of life passed with its joys and sorrows. There were many moments of indescribable tranquility. Jesus gazed on Mary and Joseph and they gazed on him. The whole family was focused on God the Father. Those were thirty years of happiness amid the most commonplace work performed with the greatest spiritual union.

831   If I should become a martyr and "give myself up to be burnt at the stake"; if I were to be an apostle preaching with "the greatest eloquence imaginable"; if I engaged in charitable works and gave "all that I have to

feed the poor…but lack charity it would avail me nothing" (cf. 1 Cor 13:2–3). It is not so much what you do
that matters, but how you do it.

832   In the present moment you may either do your own
will or the will of God. Which way will you choose?

CHAPTER 33

Leadership

The leader is one who willingly serves others.

833   A leader is needed on the Road of Hope. The leader is literally the one who leads the way. He or she may also be called the chief, that is, the head. Without the head, the limbs of the body would grow feeble, good will would be stifled, energy would dissipate, chaos would dominate, and the task at hand would come to utter ruin.

834   The leader is one who knows, desires, and carries out a mission and who simultaneously stimulates others to know, desire and carry out that mission.

835   The leader is one who serves God and those whom he or she leads. The leader is at the service of all, and wishes to be a servant.

836   Jesus cast fire on the earth and he desires the earth to be set ablaze with its brilliant light (cf. Lk 12:49).

You must be the bright flame kindled by apostolic zeal; from your bright light other torches must be kindled until the whole world is a vast sea of living flame.

837   If God chooses you to be the leader in a situation, always be humble and generous. You have a mission of supreme importance. Remember the apostles' happiness when they heard the Lord's words: "Follow me, and I will make you fish for people!" (Mk 1:17).

838   You must believe in your mission. You must draw others to it by communicating your conviction and zeal.

839   If you cannot overcome a spirit of pessimism, a despondent attitude, or a shy disposition, do not be a leader.

840   The leader is the visible sign of authority. The leader has to be mindful of his or her mission to command, to exercise authority and enable others to respect that authority. This is what is meant by serving people.

841   The greatest failure in leadership is for the leader to be afraid to speak and act as a leader.

842   Welcome all opinions, but do not depend only on opinions.

843   Only those with appropriate and effective initiative should lead.

844   Bring all the faculties of your mind to bear on making a decision, then make it bravely and at the opportune moment.

845   Countless opinions without a decision are useless. A true leader is one who has a few ideas which are carried out to completion.

846   Know what you want and desire it wholeheartedly. If you lack firm conviction, you will paralyze your co-workers. If you allow each of your co-workers the freedom to make the final decisions, you will breed chaos.

847   The leader observes a disciplined life, seeks to understand the responsibility of authority, and acts accordingly. The leader carries out plans and vigorously overcomes the obstacles that arise.

848   Your criticism of superiors dampens zeal and creates division among co-workers. It also opens the way for them to be critical of your methods and to find fault with you.

849   There is no activity which does not involve carrying the cross. If you cannot carry the cross, you will not be able to do anything at all.

850   If you wish to be a clear-headed leader, you will need to learn how to rest. To know how to relax is essential if you want to avoid impetuosity, mental fatigue, moodiness, loss of self-control, and panic.

851   A leader must be brave and calm in the face of unexpected events, whenever or wherever they may come. If the leader achieves these qualities, the severest of challenges will be overcome.

852   Overwork leads to the inability to achieve anything; over-anxiety can lead to insanity. However busy you are, you should set aside some time for reflection, study, and especially prayer. In fact the busier you are, the greater your need for reflection, study, and prayer. Through this, you will find peace.

853   Do not waste a single moment, do not utter a single superfluous word, do not waste a single opportunity. If you do this, you will improve your judgment, become more determined, and gain greater respect and admiration from others.

854   Learn how to maintain personal discipline, organize your life, and discern the value of every action. These are the conditions that will help you to be a leader who can proudly and heroically restore confidence when everyone is panic-stricken and apprehensive.

855   See things the way they are: clearly, truly, and correctly. This is the kind of realistic mind you must have in order to be a leader who relies on objective facts.

856   Set formulas are mechanical and mindless. It is useless to be weighed down by procedures, and getting lost in small details is narrow-minded. You must take an overall view of situations and be flexible at all times.

You will need advisers, experts, and especially your own resolute will.

857 You must develop and cultivate your talents so that you may be able to serve more efficiently.

858 If you are a leader who lacks the ability to lead, you will not only suffer the loss of prestige, but you will also lack credibility.

859 Do not demand that your leader possess every conceivable talent, because you will never find such an ideal leader. However, if you should become a leader, you will have to develop your talents to the fullest.

860 In order to direct every activity and focus every effort, a leader must have the ability to discern general ideas clearly in order to obtain a complete picture and an adequate knowledge of all the details of an organization.

861 Each individual person is a mystery. If you wish to be a leader, you will need to know all your co-workers, their needs, their interests, their temperaments, and their reactions. You will also need to make an exact assessment of their abilities and determine the right position for each one.

862 As Jesus lived with his apostles for three years, you should also associate with your co-workers. Be compassionate toward them, share their confidences, their joys, their sorrows, and try to understand the way each

one thinks. If you do this, you will be surprised to find how united they will become and how they will strive for excellence.

863 Try to put yourself in the position of your co-workers. Exchange points of view with them as a friend, treat them warmly, let them see that you are interested in them, and that you understand them. Such a kindly attitude will inspire them to love and trust you.

864 The honors you receive will not be medals to hang on your chest, citations to frame for your walls, or laudatory speeches. Your work as a leader will be etched in the hearts and on the faces of your co-workers.

865 If you win the hearts of your co-workers they will follow you energetically and devotedly, because they know that you love them sincerely and deeply, and that you would willingly make sacrifices for them. If you do not lead them with love you will have to employ the worst method — force.

866 To win over the hearts of co-workers, the leader must dare to allow them to share closely in his or her work, and to have confidence in his or her authority. The leader must be humble with co-workers, yet retain the dignity of his or her position, mix with them informally while retaining their respect, and request obedience from all when decisions have been made.

867 Do not forget that your co-workers are human. They are individuals and children of God, so only God

has absolute authority over them. They should not be thought of as mere possessions or productive machines.

868   The humble leader who has a sense of social responsibility, works in view of a future successor. Strive for permanence in your work, not in your personal reputation.

869   The leader whose actions contradict his or her words may be obeyed, but he or she will not be respected. The leader whose conduct is exemplary in the performance of the duties of office may be respected, but not necessarily loved. But the leader who gives a shining example in every aspect of his or her activities will be obeyed, respected, and loved — and have a far-reaching influence.

870   The mark of a great leader is that he or she knows how to recruit co-workers by seeking them, discovering them, welcoming them, choosing them, training them, trusting them, employing them, loving them. There is no ideal leader any more than there is an ideal co-worker.

871   God must be the sole guide in all leadership. As the source of true leadership, he will not fail to support those whom he calls to share his authority. True leadership is founded in a spirit of humility and charity as shown in the Gospel.

872   The leader does not only rely on reports concerning his or her co-workers, but he or she also studies them

firsthand, reads their hearts, knows their abilities, and understands their trials.

873   Jesus did not try to effect an immediate change in the apostles by issuing orders. Rather, he gave them time to be converted. Be self-confident and help others to have confidence in your mission. Live in such a way that others want to imitate you.

874   Jesus did not win followers by commands or by setting up a school of spirituality. He taught his apostles from their real-life situations, for example, the lessons to be learned from the vineyard, the wheat field, from little children, and even from their disputes among themselves (cf. Mt 21:18; Lk 9:46; Jn 4:35).

875   Although Jesus did teach some particular formal lessons, he seemed to prefer more informal encounters. Such unexpected moments brought grace to Zaccheus, Simon, and the Samaritan woman (cf. Mt 26:6 ff.; Lk 19:1 ff.; Jn 4:7).

876   Jesus did not reject the apostles because of their failure to understand him or their obstinacy. Do not be discouraged, but be patient and kind to those who may be cruel, malevolent, or selfish toward you. God's grace will eventually win them over.

877   There are many families and communities that speak only the language of mere words with each other. If they would learn to speak seriously, heart to heart, they would come closer together.

878 When conversing with Peter, Jesus did not silence his impetuosity. People's angry outbursts will not cause the world to collapse. Do not be afraid — keep talking heart to heart with others instead of arguing with them.

879 Where will you find the guiding principle for dialogue that liberates hearts to be open to others, and frees minds for wisdom and perception? You will find it in the Gospel.

880 Jesus did not turn away anyone who wished to speak to him. He spoke with friends, strangers, Gentiles, sinners, and even his enemies.

881 To be a good leader you must become all things to all people in every situation. Good leadership demands a readiness for every kind of task, fatigue, opposition, and, if necessary, the sacrifice of your life for the benefit of others. However, always be mindful of your own spiritual needs.

882 When you assume the responsibilities of leadership, remember that even after you have achieved success in the task at hand, you should still regard yourself as a useless servant and recognize that you still have many faults and failings. And do not be surprised or annoyed when the response to your efforts is only misunderstanding and ingratitude (cf. Lk 17:10).

CHAPTER 34

Examination
of Conscience

Review your life in the light of the Gospel.

883   While traveling along the Road of Hope, you will
have to stop occasionally under the shade of a tree to
review your progress. Thus you will draw upon your
experience in order to advance further and make any
necessary adjustments.

884   The greater the task, the more careful you should
be. Carelessness indicates that you have little concern
for your eternal life.

885   Looking at the past to lament it is useless. Looking
at the past to be proud of results is dangerous. Looking
at the past to learn from it is wise.

886   Your examination of conscience must be thorough,
sincere, and courageous. Just as in financial statements

one does not present an accountant with misleading information of expenses and income, so when examining one's conscience one must allow the facts of one's conduct to speak for themselves and be ready to accept the balance-sheet as it truly is.

887   Examine your conscience every night, every week, every time you celebrate the sacrament of Reconciliation, and whenever you spend time in recollection. However good a car may be, it needs a tune up at certain times. No matter how good your health is, you will still need periodic check-ups to prevent some conditions that may have no cure.

888   Do not overlook your small acts of infidelity. A terrible tempest or flood is not necessary to wreak havoc; tiny insects can destroy overnight the lush field which required the investment of money and labor.

889   Only foolish soldiers turn their backs on the enemy to avoid head wounds. Yet, this is how you behave when you disregard small sins, thinking that it is only essential to avoid serious sin.

890   You are sorrowful because of the many times you have betrayed the Lord, and rightly so. But that is not enough. You have to be like the sinful woman, who was "forgiven, and so she has shown great love" (Lk 7:47), like the disciple who ran away from the garden of Gethsemane, but later returned to stand by the cross. Be resolved to always love in action as well as word.

891   If you fail to try avoiding even small sins, your love of God will weaken and you will not have enough interior motivation to persevere along the Road of Hope.

892   A failure to examine your conscience can be a sin of omission; this is a serious matter indeed. It can lead to indifference in doing God's work, loss of the spirit of sacrifice, skill in avoiding responsibility, acting from "worldly" motives, developing a habit of avoiding the difficult path while looking for the easier one to follow.

893   Repentance and purpose of amendment should not be like acting in an opera — weeping sorrowfully according to your role in the play, but when the drama comes to an end and the curtain falls, you revert to your real self.

894   The spacecraft soars out in space, but the flight path has been clearly planned. The pilot constantly adjusts navigational equipment in response to the instructions received from earth. If the controls are handled incorrectly, the craft will not reach its goal.

895   If you simply examine the engine of a car without making necessary repairs, the car will not run well. So too, no matter how carefully you examine your conscience, if you are not resolved to amend your life, it will be of no benefit to you.

896   When examining your conscience, concentrate realistically on a few practical points. Many nebulous resolutions will not help you to amend your life or help you to become holy.

897   "Leave it till later" is sometimes a wise response, but it is more often an excuse used by the procrastinator, the fainthearted, or the disillusioned.

898   The present moment alone is important. Do not recall what your neighbor did yesterday in order to criticize it, or recall what happened to you today to weep over it; it is now in the past. Do not be pessimistic about tomorrow; it is still in the future. Entrust the past to the mercy of God, entrust the future to his providence, and entrust everything to his love.

899   Do not be sad or discouraged — this can be the result of pride. Why are you so convinced that you belong to one of the nine choirs of angels and are incapable of sinning?

900   You have dedicated yourself to be the Lord's apostle, but you do not trust him unconditionally. How can you be an effective instrument in his hands if you do not hand over the whole instrument?

901   In the face of an enormous task, you may be tempted to rely on temporal power rather than on God in order to attain quicker results for his glory. Is it for the glory of God or for your own reputation? If power were necessary, Jesus would have used it. "But first seek the kingdom and the will of God and all those things will be given to you also" (Mt 6:33). Why do you

criticize others for relying on "worldly" influence while depending on it yourself and becoming its slave?

902 Are you afraid that clever people will laugh at you for being naïve? When Teresa of Avila, Francis of Assisi, Joseph Cottolengo, and John Bosco were alive, many people called them crazy, but today these "foolish" people are honored as saints. Have confidence in God and keep pressing forward toward your goal in faith.

903 In order to head off in the right direction on the Road of Hope, you must respond at once: "Lord, all for love of you, all for you in the person of my neighbor. I do not desire to reserve anything for myself. I do not desire anyone to thank me. I do not desire any reward."

904 Having examined your conscience, what should you do? You must humbly weep for your sins as Peter did, sit at the Lord's feet and return his love as Mary of Bethany, resolve to reform as Zaccheus, and be a zealous apostle like Paul. In this way you will advance along the road filled with hope (cf. Mt 26:75; Lk 7:38–48, 19:1–10; 2 Cor 11:22–33).

905 Everyone desires books and magazines to read, schools for education, communities in which to live, employment. But hope simply remains hope as long as you depend solely on yourself. Yet, when you allow your desires to be shaped by God's grace, then they will be realized to a degree you could not have imagined.

906   The means at your disposal are the same as those the apostles had: the Blessed Eucharist, "I will be with you all the days until the end of the age" (Mt 28:20); the Holy Spirit, "He will give you another Intercessor to be with you forever" (Jn 14:16); Mary, "Here is your Mother" (Jn 19:27); the Gospel, "Go into the whole world and proclaim the good news to all creation" (Mk 16:15). Jesus has given you all this. Why do you consider it of so little worth? Does the world have anything to compare with it?

907   Your plans seem too vast, your program enormous, the obstacles confronting you as high as mountains, as wide as the sea. You wonder how, in your frailty, you can overcome them. Long ago, in times as troublesome as your own, Paul told his Christians, "God chose…the weak of the world to shame the strong" (1 Cor 1:27), and "through the grace of God I am what I am, and the grace he gave me has not been without result" (1 Cor 15:10) — that is, provided you are faithful to the inspiration of God's grace.

908   Examination of conscience means that you review your life in the light of faith.

909   Every six months, make a summary of your activities, an inventory of your belongings, and examine yourself on any changes in your desires. Make a thorough judgment of all of these and courageously dispose of those things which are useless.

CHAPTER 35

Mary

Although she was poor, she gave us
her greatest treasure — our Lord Jesus Christ
himself, our Redeemer, the giver of all graces.

910 No matter how a person may try to reassure a child, if his mother is not there, he will refuse to go along. However, with his mother, he will go through a forest, cross a stream, whether hungry or cold. During times of war, many a mother has died with her child still clinging to her. On the Road of Hope, hold on to Mary's hand. God has given her to you as your Mother; you are not alone. She is "our life, our sweetness, and our hope" *(Salve Regina).*

911 The little child wants her mother. When her mother is away, the child sobs until she returns. If you give her candy, a beautiful present, or some valuable toy, she will throw them all down and will only be happy again when she sees her mother. You must become childlike in order to get to know and love Mary.

912   The love of our Mother Mary is like a cool breeze or a drop of morning dew. It brings sweetness and consolation to the restless soul longing for peace.

913   "Here is your Mother" (Jn 19:27). After the institution of the Blessed Eucharist, the Lord could not have left us anything greater than Mary. She has crushed the head of the serpent. She will help you to conquer the devil, "the flesh," and "the world." She will obtain for you the graces to hold firm to the noble ideal which the Lord has placed in your heart.

914   No matter how tepid, sinful, or hopeless you may feel, entrust yourself into the hands of Mary. Jesus bequeathed her to you; how could she abandon you?

915   When you fall, weep humbly with her, because sin caused the death of her Son. She will receive you. She accepted the good thief as much as John. She will also accept you as her child.

916   Mary is like a popular, pocket-sized, living book of the Gospels, which is more readily accessible to you than the lives of all the saints.

917   If you desire to understand what a wonderful Mother you have, call to mind that she is the Mother of the supreme and almighty Second Person of the Holy Trinity. You are blessed indeed, because she is also your Mother. If Jesus had not told you, you could never have known this beautiful mystery.

918 If you wish to become a saint, be childlike. A child does not understand theory, but he watches his mother and follows her example. He believes that his mother knows everything and does everything correctly. So look at your Mother Mary; imitate her and you will become a saint.

919 The Litany of the Blessed Virgin Mary is like a simple book in which the Church teaches you to understand various attributes of Mary: powerful, merciful, amiable. The more you consider her, the greater will be your joy and hope in your present struggle. Like a child you will call on Mary: "Pray for us! Pray for us!"

920 The life of Mary is summed up in three words: *Ecce, Fiat,* and *Magnificat.* With spiritual fervor, impress them on your heart, ponder them, and act on them: "Behold, the handmaid of the Lord," *Ecce.* "let it be done to me according to your word," *Fiat* (Lk 1:38). "My soul gives praise to the Lord," *Magnificat* (Lk 1:46).

921 The first reaction of a child in distress is to call out, "Mommy, Mommy!" The word "Mommy" means everything to a child. In the same way, you should frequently call on Mary: "Mother, Mother! I love you. I put my trust in you. You are my all."

922 The Rosary is the chain which connects you to Mary. It is your commemorative film of her journey along the Road of Hope. It recalls her love at Bethlehem, her anxiety in Egypt, her silent labor in the carpenter's shop at Nazareth, and her fervor in the temple. You share her feelings as the Lord preached. The Rosary helps you to reflect on her suffering beside the cross, her joy at the resurrection, and her fidelity as an apostle at the side of John. To sum up, we can say: "Our Lord lives in his Mother and she in him, the two lives are one. Do not abandon the Rosary, which Mary has given and recommended to you, so that you may live like her, with her, through her, and in her."

923   There is no gift as precious as that which came to us from the heart of Mary. She gave us the Lord Jesus Christ, the most precious of gifts. Precious too, is the heart of Mary, because "blessed is the fruit of her womb, Jesus" (cf. Lk 1:42).

924   Jesus has clearly shown us that the example we are to follow is God: "So you be perfect as your heavenly Father is perfect" (Mt 5:48). Then, since no one has seen the heavenly Father, Jesus tells you where to find him — in Jesus himself, "Whoever has seen me has seen the Father" (Jn 14:9). In order to help us live like him, our Lord gave us the gentle and loving example of his mother Mary, "Here is your mother" (Jn 19:27).

925   Even if confronted with dangers and difficulties, the little child will still imitate his mother in everything. He does not actually set out to follow her example because he necessarily understands she is right about every-thing, but simply because he loves and trusts her. The

little child watches his mother take medicine and then does likewise. Mary is the shining example within your reach; imitate her. The Blessed Trinity has not created anyone holier than Mary.

926　Mary gives us an example of a modest and secluded life. Yet, she was always accessible to others. She kept a low profile, living quietly in the background, but always for Jesus. Do you live wholly for the Lord who lives in you?

927　Jesus continues to live and act in the Church and in you. Likewise, Mary is present in the Church and to you, because she is Mother of the Church and your Mother.

928　During the most glorious events of our Lord's public life — his transfiguration on Mount Tabor and his entry into Jerusalem — Mary remained hidden. But at times of gravest danger — the flight into Egypt, the way of the cross to Calvary, her sorrowful watch at the foot of the cross, and her vigil in the upper room with the apostles — Mary courageously chose to be present. She did not live for herself, but only for the Lord and his work of redemption.

929　Mary joined in prayer with the apostles, preparing herself and assisting them for the coming of the Holy Spirit. Thus she prepared for and witnessed the day of the public inauguration of the Church. In giving birth to the Lord Jesus, she gave birth to his body, the Church. Truly, she is Mother of the Church.

930   Our Blessed Mother could choose to appear in great cities or in cathedrals, or to an important person or theologian. But instead she chooses to appear to simple people in obscure places, because she likes to visit those no one else seeks out, those places people do not care to visit. And she also wishes you to come to her.

931   Mary lacked everything we would regard as necessary for happiness. When you recite the *Magnificat,* you read her words which describe her as the lowliest of the low, the servant, the humble one, the one who is hungry. However, the Lord looked into that poverty and, in his mercy, made her "full of grace" (Lk 1:28).

932   Mary was poor, having neither money nor possessions. At times she was homeless. She did not preach, but she gave the most precious Word to the shepherds at Bethlehem, to the Magi from the East, to Simeon and Anna in the temple, and to humanity on Calvary (cf. Mt 2:11; Lk 2:16, 22–39; Jn 19:25–27). Silently she gave them Jesus, the gift she alone had to offer. This gift preaches on her behalf, because this gift is the Word of God.

933   Mary's total sacrifice was ennobled because of her complete trust in God. Contrary to the custom of her time, she vowed to remain a virgin. God, however, bestowed on her the gifts of virgin motherhood and of being the Mother of God and the Mother of all people.

934   You may be great-hearted, but your pockets may be limited. Still, there is only one gift you can always give that will satisfy your desires. It is a precious gift which no one can buy, a gift beyond compare. Give the Lord Jesus Christ as Mary did.

935   With tear-filled eyes you go to Mary, Consoler of the Afflicted. When calamity strikes, you go to her who is the Help of Christians; sinful, you go to her as the Refuge of Sinners. You should become another Mary, welcoming all who come to you seeking refuge. You, also, should be "their life, their sweetness, and their hope" *(Salve Regina).*

936   Mary lived completely for Jesus. Her mission was to share in his work of Redemption. All her honor derives from him. If it were not for the fact that her Son is the Lord Jesus Christ, and that her whole life was lived for him, Mary would be nothing at all. Likewise, your own life will amount to nothing at all if you separate yourself from Jesus.

937   Value a spiritual life and find its real meaning in Mary. She was active, but her every gesture and thought, down to the smallest detail, was for Jesus. It was impossible for her to live a single moment apart from him. Her life was one of deepest interiority. In her, action is joined to contemplation. Contemplative in the midst of activity, her activity flows from her contemplation.

938   When Jesus "overcame the world" in the most bitter of conflicts between good and evil, Mary witnessed the greatest revolution known in history. Jesus did not

come to overturn, eliminate, or destroy the law, but to bring it to perfection. Mary was at his side at that historic moment when, by his sacrificial death, the Old Covenant gave place to the New.

939   If you love adventure, imitate Mary. Her life was an adventurous journey in faith. She always entrusted everything to God's hands. She followed his will always, whether at the manger, in Egypt, in Nazareth, or on Calvary. Always and everywhere she believed and persevered in faith, risking everything, yet secure in her belief that God is faithful to his promise.

940   Wherever you may be, follow the example of Mary. Imitation of Mary is not contingent on any particular place, on your being with her in the stable with the shepherds. It depends on your letting Jesus live in you through your life of charity, and on your union with him. Your life should be one continual Christmas, giving Jesus to everyone.

941   If you are a young person who wishes to live very faithfully, imitate Mary. In her there is nothing selfish. Mary is immaculate and filled with the Spirit of the Lord, so we cannot think of her without also thinking of Jesus.

942   Without God you would feel completely empty, lonely, and miserable. Attaining a satisfying level of human happiness depends on the degree of your communication with God. Mary's life was completely ori-

ented toward God. She is his perfect creation according to his will.

943 Mary is the personification of poverty itself. She was happy in freely living a life of poverty. She loved living this life of poverty because her heart was rich and her treasure was great. She was the poorest but the most beautiful mother, with the beauty bestowed on her by the Lord Jesus Christ. She may have been the poorest, but she was as beautiful as nature — lovely as the moon, radiant as the sun, shining as a dewdrop, lovable as the sparrow, fragrant as a lily in the field.

944 Mary's suffering increased even more when she felt powerless. As she watched her beloved Son from the foot of the cross, she was completely powerless. The more she loved, the more brokenhearted she became. Nevertheless, she stood firm in order to strengthen and console you whenever you feel powerless in your sufferings.

945 At the foot of the cross Mary attained a heroic exercise of meekness, humility, silence, patience, faith, hope, and love. She was poor in her loneliness, because she lost her only son, Jesus, God made man. She loved God to the point of offering her whole life in union with the blood of her Son to redeem humanity. She is a martyr. Though she could not die with her Son, she was united with his death. In the face of a purely human understanding of Jesus' death as the end of his mission and a complete, utter failure, Mary stood firm in her faith.

946   When she lost the child Jesus in the temple, Mary
suffered in her heart as she searched for him, but during
that time her love was manifested very clearly (cf. Lk
2:48). When you are no longer protected within a safe
and secure environment, and it seems that the Lord is
absent, that is the moment in which the genuineness of
your love for him can be shown.

947   Love for our Lady is clearly shown by those who
love the Rosary. Only those who love her could repeat
the same story and the same words over and over again
without becoming bored.

948   Mary was not only concerned for the Lord, but also
for Elizabeth, John, and the couple at Cana. Imitate
Mary's attitude; have consideration for our Lord, but
also for your neighbor.

CHAPTER 36

Hope

Be ready to explain to others
the hope that is in you.

949   "Blessed be the God and Father of our Lord Jesus Christ! In his great mercy we have been reborn to a living hope through the resurrection of Jesus Christ from the dead" (1 Pet 1:3).

950   Christians are a light in the darkness, the salt where life no longer has taste, and hope in the midst of a humanity which has lost hope.

951   Paul always counseled his Christians not to live like people without hope (cf. Thes 4:12).

952   As Christians "we await our blessed hope — the appearance in glory of our great God and of our Savior Christ Jesus" (Titus 2:13).

953   Many Christians leave the work of salvation to God. They fail to realize that God has entrusted the task of the salvation of the world to their collaboration.

954   To be deeply imbued with the love of God is to be deeply imbued with a love of the world. To hope in God is to hope in the salvation of the world.

955   You must proclaim the Gospel to the world. This Gospel is not a list of prohibitions; it is the extraordinary message of God's love for us. God loved and redeemed the world.

956   On the cross the Lord was very poor. Ask our crucified Lord Jesus for these only: love, suffering, and always, hope.

957   If your reflection on these pages does not help the Gospel to inundate your whole life, and you pray instead: "May thy kingdom *not* come!", you will not be the hope of the world.

958   In the last few decades humanity has made greater technological and scientific advances than it had in previous centuries. Terrible power, in the form of nuclear weapons, has been developed which could bring about the world's destruction. Humanity has everything at its disposal; nothing more seems to be required. Humanity believes it can do anything, but it does not know the meaning of life, where it is going or what the future will hold. It is experiencing a crisis of hope.

959   God does not retreat before human progress. On the contrary, the more humanity grows in power, the more it will need hope to make further progress. And the more it makes progress, the more humanity will need love to go on living. Otherwise, what is the purpose of life? Is it worthwhile? Are nihilism and hatred the heritage of human progress?

960   Some think that the more science advances, the more religion will recede. In the hearts of many, "God is dead." They think their consciences are liberated, but such liberty fills them with confusion and panic. They lack hope.

961   In every age certain people have declared themselves prophets, but their policies have not brought hope to humanity. Only Jesus proclaims himself to be "the Way"; only he offers hope with worldwide dimensions when he commands: "Go into the world and proclaim the good news to all creation" (Mk 16:15) and "you will receive power and you will be my witnesses in Jerusalem, and in all Judea and Samaria, all the way to the end of the earth" (Acts 1:8).

962   Humanity hopes to live and to go on living, and so it turns to whoever offers it the greatest hope. Jesus gives this hope: "I have come that you might have life and have it abundantly" (Jn 10:10). Mary is our model in hope; she *is* "our hope" *(Salve Regina).*

963   Lay people: love the mission you are called to live in "the world." By that mission you help to make eter-

nity present in time. You believe that God has entrusted the world and your neighbors to you, that you may be instruments leading others to eternal salvation. You firmly trust that God alone gives salvation, but that in this work he asks for human cooperation. Practice the virtue of hope, guarantee hope, and bring hope to others.

964   The person of hope is a person of prayer. The object of one's hope is also the object of prayer. The person of hope is God's collaborator. God looks to that person to complete his work of creation and redemption.

965   We pray to God but he relies on us. He established the Church as the instrument of salvation. The Church bears the responsibility for carrying out God's work and represents the greatest hope for every one of us (cf. *Ad Gentes* 1a).

966   There are Christians who sit back, fold their arms, and wait for hope to come along. They passively shirk responsibility. They look up only when they need to cry for help. In the meantime, they look neither ahead (toward making personal progress) nor around themselves (to see if they could share and shoulder the burdens of others). Hope lies within them, if only they could see it!

967   Do not keep running away from your present situation, looking to escape to a different way of life. If you "believe in life everlasting" *(Apostles' Creed),* the spirit of hope will always bud within you and will continue to flower forever.

968   Live completely in the present, but also live completely in eternity. Concern yourself with the salvation of your neighbor, but do not forget that you do this with God and for God. Work with all your might to make progress, but rely also on light from heaven. Dedicate yourself to the world with a love that is spiritual. If you do not bear great hope in your heart, what meaning does life have?

969   Help Catholics to believe in their vocations as Christians, as members of a family, as husbands and wives, in their vocations to the various occupations in which they are engaged. Then they will be filled with hope, because they will realize that their Divine Savior, who has called them, will lead them to their goal.

970   Concentrate wholly on things of the Spirit. Resolve not to divorce Catholic life from its cultural milieu; instead, help Catholics to enrich that milieu with their own spirit of hope.

971   If you should fall momentarily in your weakness, do not give up. Ask God's forgiveness and press on. In boxing tournaments, athletes frequently succumb to blows and injuries, but they keep rising to their feet. They keep hoping and finally carry off the prize.

972   Can you imagine a Christian *not* anxious to bring hope to the world?

973   To the youth of today: "Be young people of hope, because if you have hope you will always be happy, and

you will then be able to share that happiness with others" (Chiara Lubich).

974   You may be wondering when you can submit your resignation as an apostle and be able to rest. Your apostolate may vary according to your ability and age, but you accepted your apostolic mission through your Baptism and Confirmation. Only on the cross could Jesus say, "All has been fulfilled" (Jn 19:30). So also only at your death will your mission as an apostle end.

975   Families are the future and hope of the Church. We should mobilize all the strength of our Catholic families to heed the call of the Church and proclaim the Good News to the world, a world in which more and more people are failing to practice their religion.

976   Hope always: do not be discouraged by internal difficulties directly related to the apostolate. As Paul wrote: "Some proclaim Christ out of jealousy and contentiousness, but others proclaim him out of good will, and these do it out of love, because they know I am here for having defended the gospel. Those who proclaim Christ out of jealousy do so insincerely in the hope of causing me trouble while I am in prison. What does it matter? The important thing is that one way or another Christ is proclaimed, whether from false or sincere motives, and for that I rejoice" (Phil 1:15–18).

977   Do not lose hope because you lack resources. As one cardinal said, "Use the same means as the apostles. They had no machines to rely on. They preached and

wrote letters, and with such measures they conquered the world." If you can't see the truth behind this statement, perhaps your outlook is not apostolic enough.

978   A straight line consists of millions of points joined together. Likewise, a lifetime consists of millions of seconds and minutes joined together. If every point along the line is rightly set, the line will be straight. If every minute of a life is good, that life will be holy. The Road of Hope is paved with small acts of hope along life's way. A life of hope is born from every minute of hope in one's lifetime.

CHAPTER 37

A Life of Hope

*To summarize the ideas that you have
considered in this book, I hope that every day
you will recall the following simple points
as signposts on your Road of Hope.*

979   You desire to carry out a revolution: namely, to reform the world. You will carry out this precious and noble mission God has entrusted to you by the power of the Holy Spirit. Every day prepare for a new Pentecost around you.

980   Press ahead with the personal campaign to bring happiness to others. Sacrifice yourself continually with Jesus for the intention of bringing peace to people and prosperous development to nations. This is a quiet and realistic way to practice your religion.

981   Hold firmly to this apostolic ideal: "to lay down your life for your friends" because "greater love than

this no one has" (cf. Jn 15:13). Ceaselessly spend your energy and be ready to wear yourself out in winning your neighbor for God.

982   Cry out one message: "Unity for all" — that is, unity among Catholics, unity among Christians, and unity among nations, "as the Father and Son are one" (cf. Jn 17:22–23).

983   Believe in one power — the Blessed Eucharist, the Body and Blood of our Lord which give you life. "I have come that you might have life and have it abundantly" (Jn 10:10). As the manna fed the Israelites on their way to the Promised Land, so will the Eucharist nourish you as you travel along the Road of Hope (cf. Jn 6:49–50).

984   Clothe yourself in one garment and speak one language — charity. Charity is the sign by which you will be recognized as one of our Lord's disciples (cf. Jn 13:35). It is a badge that costs little but is difficult to find. Charity is the most important language of all. Paul regarded it as far more important than being able to "speak both human and angelic tongues" (cf. 1 Cor 13:1). It will be the only language used in heaven.

985   Hold firmly to one guiding principle — prayer. Nobody is stronger than the person who prays, because the Lord has promised to grant everything to that person. When you are united with one another in prayer, Christ is present among you (cf. Mt 18:20). I earnestly encourage you to set aside quality time each day for personal prayer. It will not be time wasted, I assure you! In my experience over the years I have come to better appreciate the words of Teresa of Avila: "One who does not pray does not need the devil to lead him or her astray; such a person will cast him or herself into darkness."

986   Observe one rule — the Gospel. This "constitution" is superior to all others; it is the constitution Jesus left to the apostles (cf. Mt 4:23). The Gospel is not difficult, complicated or legalistic as other constitutions often are; on the contrary, it is dynamic, gentle, and stimulating to the soul. A saint separated from the Gospel is a false saint.

987   Loyally follow one leader — Jesus Christ — and his vicar, our Holy Father the pope; likewise follow the bishops, the successors of the apostles. Live and die for the Church as Christ did. Do not forget, however, that living for the Church entails as much sacrifice as dying for the Church.

988   Nurture a special love for Mary. John Mary Vianney said: "After Jesus, my first love is Mary." Listen to her and you will not go astray; work for her and you will not fail; honor her and you will gain eternal life.

989   Take as your wisdom the science of the cross (cf. 1 Cor 2:2). Look to the cross; there you will find the solution to all the problems that worry you. If the cross is the standard by which you make your choices and decisions, your soul will be at peace.

990   Have one ideal: to turn always to God the Father, a Father who is full of love. The whole of our Lord's life, his every thought and deed, had but one aim: "the world must know that I love the Father, and just as the Father has commanded me, that is what I will do" (Jn 14:31) and "I always do what is pleasing to him" (Jn 8:29).

991   You need fear only one thing: sin.

When he was the patriarch of Constantinople, John Chrysostom incurred the wrath of the Byzantine court for his strong denunciation of sin in the Emperor's family. Various plans were suggested as a means of exacting revenge on the saint.

Plan A: Imprisonment. "But," court officials protested, "there he will have the opportunity to pray and suffer for the Lord as he has always desired."

Plan B: Banishment. "But for him, everywhere is the Lord's country."

Plan C: Death. "But then we will satisfy his desire to be a martyr…. None of these plans will cause him to suffer; on the contrary, he will joyfully accept them.

"No, there is only one thing John fears and hates above all else: sin. But it is impossible to force him to commit sin!"

If you fear sin only, no one will be stronger than you.

992   Cherish one desire: "Your kingdom come, your will be done, on earth, as it is in heaven" (Mt 6:10). Pray that on this earth those who do not yet know God will come to know him as he is known in heaven. Desire that

everyone might begin to love one another. Then will heavenly bliss truly begin on this earth. You must strive to bring this about. Begin now to share the happiness of heaven with everyone you meet in this world.

993 There is only one thing lacking: "Go sell what you have and give to the poor and you will have treasure in heaven, and come follow me" (Mk 10:21). Make up your mind once and for all. Our Lord wants volunteers who are free of other attachments.

994 Make use of the most effective apostolic method — personal contact. Enter into the lives of others to understand and to love them. Developing personal relationships is more effective than preaching and writing books. Contact between one person and another — heart-to-heart exchange — is the secret of perseverance and success.

995 Only one thing truly matters; Mary of Bethany chose the better part when she sat at our Lord's feet (cf. Lk 10:41–42). If you are not living an interior life, if Jesus is not the very life and soul of your activities, then you don't need further instruction; the consequences of such a way of living are all too clear.

996 You have only one food — the will of the Father (cf. Jn 4:34). That is, you live and grow by the will of God. Your actions must proceed from the will of God. It is like food that nourishes you with strength and happiness; apart from God's will you would die.

997   Only one moment exists for you in all its beauty, and that is the present moment (cf. Mt 6:34; Jas 4:13–15). Live it completely in the love of God. If your life is built up like a large crystal from millions of such moments, it will be a wonderfully beautiful life. Can't you see how easy it could be?

998   The only statements you must affirm and live are the eight Beatitudes (cf. Mt 5:3–12). Jesus proclaimed them in the Sermon on the Mount. Live according to the Beatitudes and you will experience a happiness that you will communicate to all you meet.

999   You have only one important work — your mission. It cannot be described as big or small, because when you perform your mission you are doing the work of your heavenly Father. He has determined that you alone are to perform this work to carry out his plan in history (cf. Lk 2:49; Jn 17:4). Many people invent complicated ways of practicing virtue and then complain how difficult it is. The performance of your mission, however, is the most certain and simplest path of virtue you can follow.

1000   There is only one way to become holy: through the grace of God and your decision to live by that grace (cf. 1 Cor 15:10). God will never withhold grace; but is your will strong enough?

1001 You have only one reward: God himself. When God told Thomas Aquinas: "You have written well of me, Thomas; what reward do you desire?" Thomas rightly replied, "Only you, Lord!"

Also available from Pauline Books and Media:

Biography of Francis Xavier Nguyễn Văn Thuận:

The Miracle of Hope:
Political Prisoner, Prophet of Peace.
The Life of Francis Xavier Nguyễn Văn Thuận

Books by Francis Xavier Nguyễn Văn Thuận:

Testimony of Hope:
The Spiritual Exercises Preached to John Paul II

The Road of Hope:
A Gospel from Prison

Prayers of Hope, Words of Courage

Five Loaves and Two Fish

BOOKS & MEDIA

The Daughters of St. Paul operate book and media centers at the following addresses. Visit, call or write the one nearest you today, or find us on the World Wide Web, www.pauline.org

CALIFORNIA
3908 Sepulveda Blvd, Culver City, CA 90230   310-397-8676
5945 Balboa Avenue, San Diego, CA 92111   858-565-9181
46 Geary Street, San Francisco, CA 94108   415-781-5180

FLORIDA
145 S.W. 107th Avenue, Miami, FL 33174   305-559-6715

HAWAII
1143 Bishop Street, Honolulu, HI 96813   808-521-2731
Neighbor Islands call: 800-259-8463

ILLINOIS
172 North Michigan Avenue, Chicago, IL 60601   312-346-4228

LOUISIANA
4403 Veterans Memorial Blvd, Metairie, LA 70006   504-887-7631

MASSACHUSETTS
885 Providence Hwy, Dedham, MA 02026   781-326-5385

MISSOURI
9804 Watson Road, St. Louis, MO 63126   314-965-3512

NEW JERSEY
561 U.S. Route 1, Wick Plaza, Edison, NJ 08817   732-572-1200

NEW YORK
150 East 52nd Street, New York, NY 10022   212-754-1110
78 Fort Place, Staten Island, NY 10301   718-447-5071

PENNSYLVANIA
9171-A Roosevelt Blvd, Philadelphia, PA 19114   215-676-9494

SOUTH CAROLINA
243 King Street, Charleston, SC 29401   843-577-0175

TENNESSEE
4811 Poplar Avenue, Memphis, TN 38117   901-761-2987

TEXAS
114 Main Plaza, San Antonio, TX 78205   210-224-8101

VIRGINIA
1025 King Street, Alexandria, VA 22314   703-549-3806

CANADA
3022 Dufferin Street, Toronto, Ontario, Canada M6B 3T5   416-781-9131
1155 Yonge Street, Toronto, Ontario, Canada M4T 1W2   416-934-3440

¡También somos su fuente para libros, videos y música en español!